COOKING
FROM ABOVE
CLASSICS

COOKING FROM ABOVE
CLASSICS

KEDA BLACK

PHOTOGRAPHY FRÉDÉRIC LUCANO • STYLING SONIA LUCANO

✳ ✳ ✳

hamlyn

First published in France in 2007 under the title
Les Basiques, by Hachette Livre (Marabout)
Copyright © 2007 Hachette Livre (Marabout)

© Text Keda Black
Photography by Frédéric Lucano
Styling by Sonia Lucano

An Hachette UK Company
www.hachette.co.uk

First published in Great Britain in 2009 by
Hamlyn, a division of Octopus Publishing Group Ltd
2–4 Heron Quays, London E14 4JP
www.octopusbooksusa.com

Copyright © English edition
Octopus Publishing Group Ltd 2009

Distributed in the United States and Canada by
Hachette Book Group
237 Park Avenue, New York, NY 10017 USA

ISBN 978-0-600-61963-5

Printed and bound in Singapore

10 9 8 7 6 5 4 3 2 1

Measurements Standard level spoon measurements
are used in all recipes.

Nuts This book includes dishes made with nuts and
nut derivatives. It is advisable for those with known
allergic reactions to nuts and nut derivatives and
those who may be potentially vulnerable to these
allergies, such as pregnant and nursing mothers,
invalids, the elderly, babies, and children, to avoid
dishes made with nuts and nut oils. It is also advisable
to check the labels of preprepared ingredients for
the possible inclusion of nut derivatives.

Eggs should be large unless otherwise stated. The
Department of Health advises that eggs should not
be consumed raw. This book contains dishes made
with raw or lightly cooked eggs. It is advisable for
more vulnerable people, such as pregnant and nursing
mothers, invalids, the elderly, babies, and young
children, to avoid uncooked or lightly cooked dishes
made with eggs. Once prepared these dishes should
be kept refrigerated and used promptly.

Milk should be full fat unless otherwise stated.

Butter is unsalted unless otherwise stated.

Fresh herbs should be used unless otherwise stated.
If unavailable use dried herbs as an alternative but
halve the quantities stated.

Ovens should be preheated to the specific
temperature—if using a fan-assisted oven, follow
manufacturer's instructions for adjusting the time
and the temperature.

FOREWORD

This book is a collection of indispensable recipes: the basics that never go out of fashion, with a modern twist (steak and French fries, roast chicken, pumpkin soup, pan-fried scallops, floating islands…), and new classics, just wonderful as they are (rabbit tagine, light moussaka, pasta with pesto, zucchini crumble, cheesecake…). Here are 80 recipes that you should master once and for all!

To ensure not a single one is ever a failure, the method is foolproof: for each crucial stage in a recipe there is a photograph. The mysteries of Béarnaise sauce, shown step by step, become clear. Every stage for preparing beef braised in beer or wine is illustrated; it's as easy as ABC. See in full color how to make real mayonnaise; how to whiz up a gazpacho in the blender; or how to incorporate flour with egg before it is blended with milk to become perfect pancake batter that spreads in the skillet before being flipped over and devoured with preserves. Delicious!

And there you have it! For the beginner cook, the essentials; for the weekend cook, more culinary know-how; and, for the advanced, great new ideas. All with photographs and every one of them simplicity itself!

CONTENTS

1
THE CLASSICS

2
PASTA & RICE

3
MEAT

4
FISH

5
VEGETABLES

6
DESSERTS

APPENDICES

CLASSICS

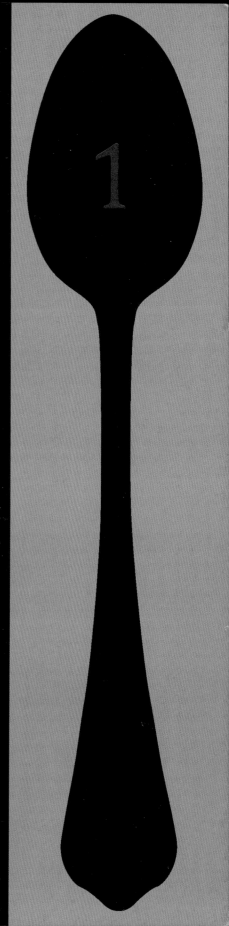

MAYONNAISE

2 egg yolks
½ teaspoon salt
½ teaspoon Dijon mustard (optional)

1¼ cups oil (one part sunflower to two parts olive oil)
½–1 teaspoon lemon juice
freshly ground pepper

FOR GARLIC MAYONNAISE:
Crush 2–5 garlic cloves with the salt in a small bowl before adding in the egg yolks.

10

1
4

2
5

3
6

1	Put the egg yolks in a large mixing bowl.	2	Add the salt and mustard.	3	Beat with a hand-held electric whisk.
4	Pour in a drop of oil and beat. Continue adding oil a drop at a time and beat until the mixture thickens.	5	After a third of the oil has been added, pour in a steady thin stream, while beating continuously.	6	Once the mayonnaise has become really thick, season with a little lemon juice and pepper.

CLASSIC FRENCH DRESSING

⋇ SERVES 4 • PREPARATION: 5 MINUTES ⋇

1 tablespoon red wine vinegar
⅛ teaspoon salt
½–1 teaspoon French mustard

3 tablespoons olive oil
a few grindings of pepper

1	Mix the vinegar with the salt then add the mustard.	2	Add the oil, a little at a time, while stirring.	3	Season with pepper.
SHAKER-STYLE ❀					
4	Put everything into a clean pickles jar.	5	Screw on the lid tightly and shake the jar.	6	It's ready.

GARLIC FRENCH DRESSING

VARIATION ON CLASSIC FRENCH DRESSING
❋

1 small garlic clove
⅛ teaspoon salt
1 tablespoon lemon juice
3 tablespoons olive oil
freshly ground pepper

Crush the peeled garlic with the salt using a pestle and mortar or a small spoon until it forms a paste.

Add the lemon juice, mix well, then stir in the oil and lightly season with pepper.

ALL LEMON FRENCH DRESSING

VARIATION ON CLASSIC FRENCH DRESSING
✳

1 tablespoon lemon juice
3 tablespoons olive oil
⅛ teaspoon salt
peel of ½ lemon

☞ Mix everything together!

VERY GREEN SALAD

❖ SERVES 4 • PREPARATION: 15 MINUTES ❖

1 head lettuce of your choice: romaine,
Boston lettuce, escarole, frisée, and so forth
French Dressing (see recipe 02)
½ bunch of chives, chopped
leaves from 4 chervil stalks, chopped

leaves from 4 tarragon stalks, chopped
fronds from 4 dill stalks, chopped
leaves from 4 mints stalks, chopped
3–4 scallions, green parts included
(optional), chopped

CUSTOMIZE YOUR DRESSING:
You can add, for example, a little crème
fraîche for romaine, some crushed blue
cheese for frisée, walnut oil for escarole...

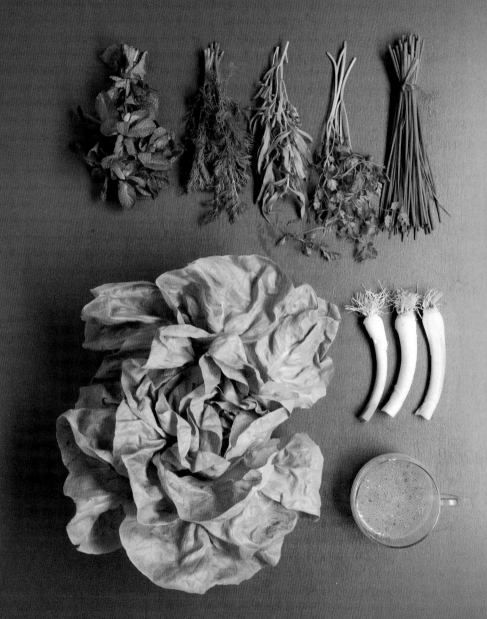

1 2
3 4

1	Remove the base of the salad leaves, discarding any outer leaves that have spoiled. Separate the good leaves and plunge into cold water.	2	Drain and repeat in clean water. Do not let the leaves remain soaking in the water. Dry them well, preferably in a salad spinner.
3	Tear up any large leaves and put them all in a large salad bowl.	4	Drizzle over the French dressing and stir to coat the leaves. Add the chopped herbs and scallions. Stir again and serve.

BÉCHAMEL SAUCE

4 tablespoons butter
⅓ cup all-purpose flour
2⅔ cups milk
salt and freshly ground pepper

pinch of freshly grated nutmeg
1 pat of butter or 1 tablespoon sour cream
(optional)

90

1	Gently melt the butter in a small pan over a medium heat.	2	Remove from the heat and tip in the flour in one go.	3	Mix with a wooden spoon.
4	Return the pan to the heat and add the milk little by little (1 tablespoon then 2 tablespoons at a time).	5	Incorporate all the milk then let the sauce cook for 7–8 minutes over a very gentle heat.	6	Season with the salt, pepper, and nutmeg. For a richer sauce, stir in the butter or sour cream.

CHEESE SOUFFLÉ

⇒ SERVES 2 • PREPARATION: 15 MINUTES • COOKING: 35 MINUTES ⇐

butter, for greasing
1¼ cups Béchamel Sauce (see recipe 06),
prepared and cooled
3 oz shredded cheese (Emmental, Monterey
Jack, or another hard variety)

pinch of cayenne pepper
pinch of caraway or cumin seeds, crushed
(optional)
3 eggs

IN ADVANCE:

Butter an 8-inch round soufflé dish.
Preheat the oven to 375°F.

1 2
3 4

1	Incorporate the shredded cheese and the spices into the just-cooled bechamel sauce.	2	Separate the eggs.	
3	Beat the egg yolks and stir into the sauce.	4	Beat the egg whites with an electric beater until they form firm peaks.	➤

	Beat in 2 tablespoons of egg white into the sauce. Fold in the remaining whites very delicately, lifting the mixture as you go, using a metal tablespoon or slotted spoon.	**GOOD TO KNOW** ✳
5		☛ A slotted spoon is a really useful tool for folding whisked egg whites into a mixture (savory or sweet). It allows you to cut through the mixture without losing all the air.

6	Carefully pour the mixture into the prepared dish and transfer to the oven. Cook for 35 minutes. Serve at once, with green salad.	**TIP** ❁ For a well-risen souffle, don't be tempted to open the oven door while it is cooking!
	TIP ❁ You can reserve a little of the shredded cheese to sprinkle over the surface. It forms a light crust which helps the soufflé underneath to rise.	**VARIATIONS** ❁ Of course, you can try different cheese varieties: a blue, or goats' cheese…

SHORT PIE PASTRY

❧ **FOR A 9-INCH TART TO SERVE 4 • PREPARATION: 15 MINUTES • RESTING: 1 HOUR MINIMUM** ❧

2 heaping cups all-purpose flour
½ teaspoon salt

8 tablespoons butter (if you use salted butter, omit the salt)
cold water to mix

PREPARE AHEAD:
Pie pastry can be made up to 2 days in advance of use. It also freezes very well.

1
4

2
5

3
6

1	Put the flour, the salt, and the butter, cut into cubes, in a large bowl.	2	Use your fingertips to rub the butter into the flour until it resembles breadcrumbs.	3	Add half a glass of cold water and mix in using a round-bladed knife.
4	The dough will combine.	5	Finish forming the dough into a ball by lightly working with your hands. On no account work it heavily.	6	Put the dough into a plastic bag or cover in plastic wrap and place in the fridge to rest for at least 1 hour.

QUICHE LORRAINE

❧ **SERVES 4** • PREPARATION: 15 MINUTES • COOKING: 50 MINUTES ❧

butter, for greasing
5 oz smoked bacon
Short Pie Pastry (see recipe 08)
3 large eggs

1¼ cups heavy cream (full- or half-fat)
pinch of freshly ground nutmeg
salt and pepper

IN ADVANCE:
Grease a 9-inch quiche pan. Preheat the oven to 350°F. Cut the bacon into small dice.

1	Brown off the bacon in a nonstick skillet.	2	Roll out the pastry and use to line the quiche pan. Prick the base with a fork then place the pan in the fridge.	3	Put the cooked bacon in the pastry-lined pan.
4	Mix the eggs with the cream and the nutmeg. Add a little salt and pepper.	5	Pour the cream mixture into the quiche pan.	6	Transfer to the oven for 35–40 minutes until the top is golden-brown.

FRESH PIZZA MARGARITA

❧ SERVES 2 • PREPARATION: 10 MINUTES • COOKING: 15 MINUTES ❧

1 lb prepared bread dough
1 cup Tomato Sauce (see recipe 20)

8 oz mozzarella, preferably made with
buffalo milk
leaves from 4 basil stalks

IN ADVANCE:
Preheat the oven to its highest setting.
Keep the bread dough in the fridge until
1 hour before you want to make the pizza.

1 2
3 4

1	Roll out the dough on a lightly floured pastry board. If it springs back too much, leave it to rest a little before rolling out further.	2	Place the dough on a baking sheet and spread with tomato sauce.
3	Tear the mozzarella into small pieces with your fingers and scatter evenly over the pizza.	4	Transfer the pizza to the oven and cook for 10–15 minutes, depending on the thickness of the base. Garnish with torn basil leaves and serve.

BOILED EGG AND SPICE BREAD

❧ SERVES 1 • PREPARATION: 5 MINUTES • COOKING: 10 MINUTES ❧

1 egg
butter
bread and spice bread to make fingers
salt

VARIATION:
Very classy: try shavings of dried salted
fish roe (sold as "poutargue" or "bottarga")
with this simple meal.

You can also use breadsticks for dipping
into the egg.

1	Place the egg in a small pan and cover with cold water.	2	Bring to the boil then cook for 3 minutes.
3	Drain and immediately open the top with a small sharp knife.	4	Serve the boiled egg with buttered fingers of bread and spice bread and a little salt.

SOFT BOILED EGG & ASPARAGUS

❖ **SERVES 1** • **PREPARATION: 5 MINUTES** • **COOKING: 13 MINUTES** ❖

1 egg
asparagus stalks, cooked
olive oil
sea salt flakes

OTHER IDEAS:

This is also delicious with an arugula salad,
with bacon, as part of a salade niçoise...

1 2
3 4

1	Place the egg in a small pan and cover with cold water.	2	Bring to the boil and cook for 6 minutes.
3	Plunge the egg into cold water, then shell.	4	Serve on a bed of asparagus stalks, with a drizzle of olive oil and the salt flakes.

CORSICAN OMELET

❖ **SERVES 1** • PREPARATION: 5 MINUTES • COOKING: 5 MINUTES ❖

3 eggs
salt and freshly ground pepper
1 tablespoon butter

2 tablespoons drained ricotta or quark cheese
leaves from 2 mint stalks

OTHER IDEAS:
Use different cheese and herbs of your choosing.

13

1	Crack the eggs, break the yolks with a fork, then season with salt and pepper.	2	Melt the butter in a small skillet over a medium-high heat. When it foams, add the beaten eggs.	3	When the base of the omelet is set, tilt the pan so that the uncooked egg runs to the sides of the hot skillet.
4	Sprinkle the cheese and torn mint leaves over the top of the omelet.	5	Fold the omelet in half, turn off the heat, and let cook for 2–4 minutes.	6	Slide out onto a plate.

SCRAMBLED EGGS

✥ **SERVES 1** • PREPARATION: 5 MINUTES • COOKING: 10 MINUTES ✥

2 tablespoons butter
4 eggs
salt and freshly ground pepper
½ bunch of chervil and ½ bunch of chive,
chopped

OTHER IDEAS:
Garnish your scrambled eggs with smoked
salmon (or with truffle shavings for the
de-luxe version), or with hot pepper sauce
and cilantro for a Mexican-style brunch.

1	Melt the butter in a small skillet over a gentle heat.	2	Crack the eggs into a bowl, mix without beating, then season with salt and pepper.
3	Tip the eggs into the pan and cook, stirring continuously with a wooden spoon, until they are set to a creamy consistency.	4	Add the chopped herbs and serve.

CLASSIC STEAK

❧ SERVES 2 • PREPARATION: 2 MINUTES • COOKING: 4 MINUTES ❧

2 beef steaks about ½ inch thick, each
weighing 7 oz
1 tablespoon olive oil
salt and freshly ground pepper

IN ADVANCE:
Lightly oil the steaks then pepper them.

IS IT COOKED?
The steak is cooked rare when it yields
slightly to the pressure of a finger—or cut it
to see if the inside is done to your liking.

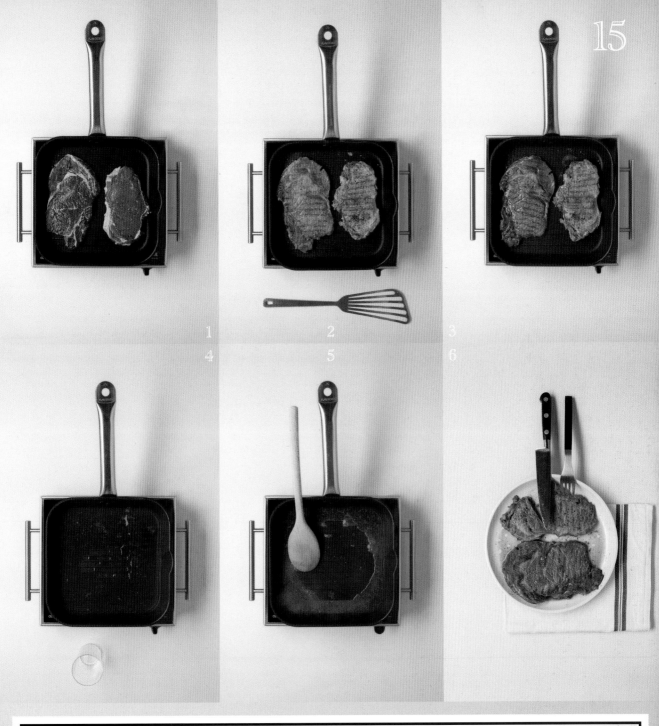

1	Preheat a heavy-based skillet. Put in the steaks, press with a fish slice, and cook for 2 minutes.	2	Turn over the steaks, season with salt, and cook again for 2 minutes, pressing down with a spatula.	3	Test the steaks are done to your liking (see the tip). Put the steak on warm serving plates.
4	Return the pan to the heat and pour in half a glass of water.	5	Scrape up any caramelized bits and let the water boil and evaporate a little.	6	Pour these cooking juices over the steaks and serve.

BÉARNAISE SAUCE

➤ **SERVES 2** • PREPARATION: 5 MINUTES • COOKING: 10 MINUTES ◄

2 small shallots
3 tablespoons tarragon vinegar or white wine
4 peppercorns
3 tarragon stalks

2 egg yolks
5 oz soft butter, cut into cubes
salt

IN ADVANCE:
Peel and finely chop the shallots.

1	Put the shallots into a small pan with the vinegar, peppercorns, and tarragon.	2	Bring to a boil, let it reduce, then remove the peppercorns and herbs.	3	Put the egg yolks in a small bowl over a pan of gently simmering water.
4	Add the reduced vinegar and whisk to combine.	5	Whisk in the butter, a cube at a time. Turn off the heat once half the butter has been added.	6	Continue to add the butter off the heat. The sauce should become rich and thick. Season with salt.

BLUE CHEESE SAUCE

→ SERVES 2 • PREPARATION: 2 MINUTES • COOKING: 5 MINUTES ←

3½ oz blue cheese
scant cup sour cream (not reduced fat)
freshly ground pepper

17

1	Put the cheese with 1 or 2 spoonfuls of the sour cream in a small pan.	2	Let melt over a gentle heat.
3	Add the remaining sour cream and bring to a boil, stirring all the time with a wooden spoon.	4	Remove from the heat when the sauce is thick enough to coat the back of the spoon. Season with pepper.

GREEN PEPPERCORN SAUCE

❧ **SERVES 2** • PREPARATION: 2 MINUTES • COOKING: 10 MINUTES ❧

½ cup white wine vinegar
1 shallot
1–1½ teaspoons green peppercorns in brine, drained

scant cup sour cream
1 teaspoon Dijon mustard
salt (optional)

1	Put the vinegar in a small pan with a small glass of water. Gently bring to a boil.	2	Chop the shallot finely and add to the boiling vinegar. Let cook for a few minutes until the liquid is reduced to 2 tablespoons. Remove from the heat.
3	Discard the shallot. Add the peppercorns to the reduction. Return the pan to the heat and add the crème fraîche and the mustard.	4	Bring to a boil. Let the sauce further reduce on a very gentle heat for 2–3 minutes. Taste and season with salt if necessary.

FRENCH FRIES

➤ SERVES 2 • PREPARATION: 15 MINUTES • COOKING: 10 MINUTES ➤

4 large floury potatoes suitable for making fries or mash
2 quarts vegetable oil
salt, to serve

USING A DEEP FRYER:
Remove the basket from the fryer. Pour in the oil and switch on the fryer. Preheat the fryer to 300°F.

TEST:
Drop one chip into the oil. If it is hot enough, the chip should rise to the surface and create small bubbles.

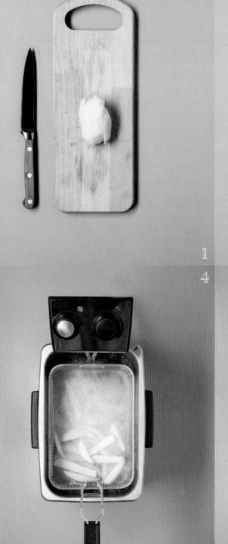

| 1 | Peel the potatoes. | 2 | Cut them into fries about ½ inch thick. | 3 | Put the fries into a large bowl of cold water to stop them turning brown. |
| 4 | Drain and dry the fries on paper towels. Place them in the basket and lower carefully into the hot oil. | 5 | Deep-fry for 5 minutes. Do not overload the fryer; it is better to cook this stage in batches if necessary. | 6 | Fry all the fries for another 3–4 minutes until golden. Drain on paper towels, sprinkle with salt and serve. |

PASTA & RICE

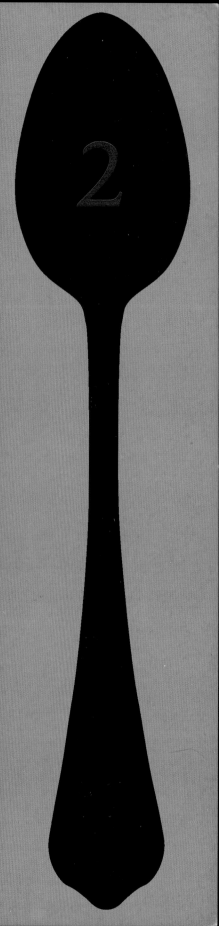

SAUCES

PASTA

RICE

CHERRY TOMATO SAUCE

❖ SERVES 2 • PREPARATION: 5 MINUTES • COOKING: 25 MINUTES ❖

1 tablespoon olive oil
1 onion, chopped
1 garlic clove, peeled, crushed, and finely chopped
1 lb cherry tomatoes

2 thyme sprigs and/or 4 basil stalks
salt and freshly ground pepper
¼ teaspoon sugar (optional)
¼ teaspoon butter (optional)

Using cherry tomatoes gives a sauce with more texture (and often more flavor) but of course you can substitute ordinary tomatoes.

1	Heat the oil in a skillet over a medium heat. Soften the onion and garlic for 5 minutes, without coloring.

OPTIONAL SPICE

❋

Sprinkle the onion and garlic with a teaspoonful of curry spices or the North African mix ras-el-hanout for a sauce that is very good with egg dishes.

TO MAKE "PIPERADE"

❋

Add 1 or 2 finely chopped red bell peppers to the onion and garlic as they soften in the skillet. At the end of cooking, add 2 eggs and stir gently as if making scrambled eggs. The result is similar to "piperade," a dish from southwest France, which is a cross between scrambled eggs and omelet.

➤

TIP

☞ If you are using ordinary tomatoes it is best to skin them first. Plunge them in boiling water for 1 minute then the skins slip off easily.

2

Add the tomatoes, the thyme and/or basil leaves, and salt and pepper. Mix well then let cook, uncovered, for 20 minutes over a low-medium heat.

NOTE

A little sugar helps the flavor of tomatoes if they haven't had enough sun to ripen fully.

3	At the end of cooking the sauce should be well reduced. Taste, adjust the seasoning, and add a little sugar if necessary.

NOTE
❈

Adding a little butter to the sauce makes it richer.

OTHER IDEAS
❈

Stir the sauce if you want it to be smooth. This sauce is good for pasta and as a pizza topping. It is delicious served with sliced eggplant cooked on the grill.
Add ⅔ cup coconut milk and a pinch of saffron threads for an excellent stock in which to cook fillets of fish or prawns.

QUICK BOLOGNAISE SAUCE

SERVES 4 • PREPARATION: 5 MINUTES • COOKING: 30 MINUTES

1 tablespoon olive oil
2 onions
1 garlic clove

3½ oz pancetta, cut into small pieces,
or use bacon slices
8 oz ground beef
14 oz canned tomatoes

1 teaspoon tomato paste
4 basil stalks
salt and freshly ground pepper

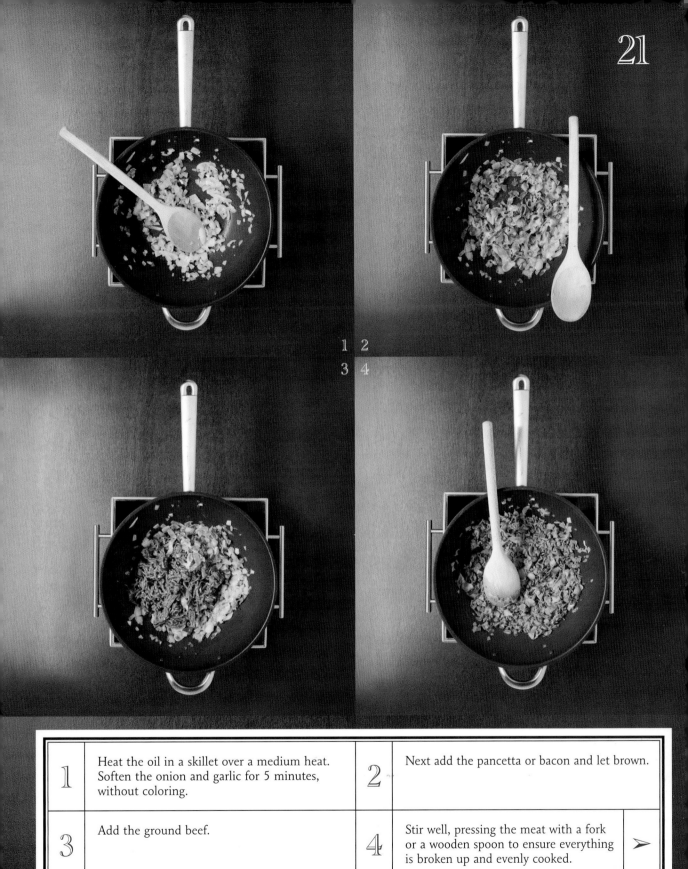

1 2
3 4

1	Heat the oil in a skillet over a medium heat. Soften the onion and garlic for 5 minutes, without coloring.	2	Next add the pancetta or bacon and let brown.	
3	Add the ground beef.	4	Stir well, pressing the meat with a fork or a wooden spoon to ensure everything is broken up and evenly cooked.	➤

5 Add the canned tomatoes, the tomato paste, and the basil leaves. Season with salt and pepper and mix well.

IN SUMMER

Use fresh tomatoes instead of canned. Skin (first plunge them into boiling water for a few minutes) and quarter them.

NOTE

Tomato paste is not essential but it does add to the depth of flavor.

IN WINTER

Select good-quality canned tomatoes; usually the Italian ones. Check the ingredients to see if they include acidifiers; those in rich juice only are best.

6	Cover the pan and let bubble gently for 20 minutes over a low heat.

VARIATIONS
❊

Instead of ground beef you can use ground pork, which children love. Or you can add a glass of hearty red wine at the same time as the tomatoes.

SERVING IDEAS
❊

Serve this sauce over tagliatelle, spaghetti, or layered in a lasagne and topped with béchamel sauce. You can also use it to stuff large zucchini: put them in the oven to roast for 25 minutes at 400°F. Sprinkle with Parmesan and return to the oven for a further 10 minutes.

22

ARUGULA PESTO

SERVES 4–6 • PREPARATION: 10 MINUTES

3½ oz arugula leaves
1 or 2 garlic cloves
2 tablespoons pine nuts
salt

1 oz shredded Parmesan or very dry Pecorino cheese
6 tablespoons olive oil

CLASSIC PESTO:
Instead of arugula, use basil, of course!

FOR A MORE UNUSUAL PESTO:
Use small tender dandelion leaves.

| 1 | Use a pestle and mortar to crush the arugula leaves with the garlic, the pine nuts, and a little salt. | **TIPS**
❀
⁕ Toast the pine nuts for 4–5 minutes in the top of a very hot oven.
⁕ For preference use green (fresh) garlic which has a more subtle flavor.
⁕ Use large grain salt or salt flakes if you can. The coarseness makes it easier to grind all the ingredients in the mortar. | ➢ |

3	Add the oil, first drop by drop, then in a thin stream, as if making mayonnaise.
2	Add the shredded cheese.

❋ TOOLS & EQUIPMENT

➤ Using a pestle and mortar requires more effort but gives a better texture than using a blender. Work in batches if your pestle and mortar is a small one.

➤ The best pestles and mortars are the heaviest: in stone (try Indian stores), in marble, and sometimes in metal. Wooden ones are less effective.

4	The pesto is ready.	**NOTE** ❋

For a lighter version you can reduce the amount of olive oil. However, if you want to keep the pesto in the fridge for a few days, you will need to cover it with a layer of oil to protect it from oxidation.

STORING
❋

The pesto will keep for a few days in the fridge stored in a well-sealed jar.

GOATS' CHEESE & PESTO TOASTS

VARIATION ON ARUGULA PESTO
❊

Spread the pesto on a toasted slice of country-style bread and top with fresh goats' cheese.

OTHER IDEAS:
This is also very good with fresh or sun-blush tomatoes.

You can use whole slices of bread or make mini toasts (sliced baguette) to serve with drinks.

PISTACHIO PESTO

VARIATION ON ARUGULA PESTO

❋

Put 3½ oz arugula leaves, 1 or 2 garlic cloves, a pinch of salt, 2 tablespoons pistachios, and 6 tablespoons oil in a blender.

Pulse until all the ingredients are fully blended. Transfer the pesto to a small bowl and add 1 oz shredded Parmesan.

NOTE:
The pistachios give a lovely green color, but you can equally use walnuts, pecan nuts, almonds…

SPAGHETTI WITH TOMATO SAUCE

❖ **SERVES 2** • **PREPARATION: 5 MINUTES** • **COOKING: 10 MINUTES** ❖

1–1¾ cups Tomato Sauce (see recipe 20)
or Bolognaise Sauce (see recipe 21)
about 7 oz dry spaghetti (according to appetite)

salt
shredded Parmesan to serve

1
4

2
5

3
6

1	Bring a large pan of salted water to a boil (allow 1¾ pints water to each 3½ oz pasta.	2	When the water reaches a full boil, add the spaghetti and then bring back to a full boil.	3	One or 2 minutes before the end of the cooking time indicated on the pack, test a strand to see if it is cooked.
4	Drain the spaghetti when it is "al dente."	5	Mix the tomato sauce into the spaghetti.	6	Serve the spaghetti sprinkled with Parmesan.

SPINACH & SQUASH LASAGNE

❧ SERVES 4 • PREPARATION: 30 MINUTES • COOKING: 1 HOUR 30 MINUTES ❧

2 small squash (Hokkaido, butternut, or Delicato)

1 lb baby spinach

¼ oz butter + extra for greasing

salt and freshly ground pepper

pinch of cayenne pepper

8 oz precooked dry lasagne

2 cups Tomato Sauce (see recipe 20 or use store bought)

7 oz ricotta

1½ oz Parmesan

1½ cups Béchamel Sauce (see recipe 06)

IN ADVANCE:

Preheat the oven to 400°F.

1	Put the squash in a roasting pan and bake in the oven for 40–50 minutes.	2	Meanwhile, wash the spinach leaves, then destalk and pick them over.	3	Put the spinach in a pan over a medium heat. Add half the butter, salt, and the cayenne.
4	Cover the pan and leave the spinach to wilt for 5 minutes.	5	Remove the squash from the oven and cut in half. Scrape out the seeds and fiber.	6	Tip the flesh into a bowl and mash in some seasoning. ➤

7 8
9 10

7	Reduce the oven temperature to 350°F. Butter a medium rectangular ovenproof dish. Line the base with a layer of lasagne.	8	Cover the lasagne with half the puréed squash then half the spinach.
9	Follow this with a layer of tomato sauce then crumble over half the ricotta.	10	Repeat the layers, first lasagne, then vegetables, tomato sauce, and the ricotta. Finish with a third layer of lasagne then pour over the béchamel and sprinkle with Parmesan shavings.

11	Bake in the oven for 30 minutes.	**ABOUT BUTTERNUT SQUASH** ❈
		Butternut is an elongated squash with a bulbous end, skin the color of egg yolk, and orange flesh. It has become very popular but you can use other varieties just as well.
	STORING ❈	
	The lasagne freezes very well.	

PASTA WITH LEMON & CREAM

➤ SERVES 4 • PREPARATION: 5 MINUTES • COOKING: 15 MINUTES ⬿

1 lemon
13 oz short-length dry pasta
4 tablespoons salted butter

scant 1 cup whipping cream, full- or reduced-fat
salt and freshly ground pepper
2½ oz Parmesan

1 2
3 4

1	Pare the lemon and squeeze the juice. Measure off 2 tablespoons of juice.	2	Cook the pasta according to the instructions on the pack.
3	Melt the butter in a small pan over a low heat. Add the cream, season, then add the lemon peel and juice. Bring gently to a boil and allow to cook for 2 minutes.	4	Drain and mix the pasta with the sauce and serve sprinkled with shredded or shaved Parmesan.

STIR-FRIED "PAD THAI" NOODLES

❧ SERVES 2 • PREPARATION: 20 MINUTES • COOKING: 5 MINUTES ❧

5 oz tofu
1 garlic clove and 2 scallions
1 small carrot
4 oz ribbon noodles (soy bean or rice)

2 tablespoons peanuts
4 tablespoons groundnut oil
2 tablespoons rice or white wine vinegar
2 tablespoons soy sauce

1½ teaspoons sugar
2 eggs
handful of beansprouts
2 large mint sprigs

1 2
3 4

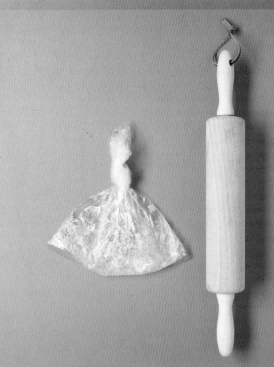

1	Cut the tofu into dice. Peel and finely chop the garlic. Trim and finely chop the scallions. Peel and shred the carrot.	2	Cover the noodles with cold water, let soak for 10 minutes, then drain.	
3	Dry-roast the peanuts in a hot skillet, shaking them constantly until they are golden.	4	Transfer the peanuts to a plastic bag and crush them with a rolling pin or a glass bottle.	➤

5 6
7 8

5	Heat a wok over a very high heat. Add the oil and fry the tofu, stirring constantly until the cubes are browned on all sides.	6	Add the garlic, noodles, carrot, vinegar, soy sauce, sugar, and ½ cup of water, stirring all the time.
7	Push these ingredients to the sides of the wok. Crack the eggs into the wok. Stir them to break the yolks then gradually incorporate them into the noodle mixture.	8	Allow to cook for 2–3 minutes, stirring and shaking the wok.

	Share out between 2 plates. Sprinkle with the crushed peanuts and arrange the beansprouts and mint sprigs on the side.	**SERVING SUGGESTION** ❋ Serve with sweet chili sauce if you like it.
9		**VARIATIONS** ❋ In place of tofu you can use strips of chicken breast or shrimp.

SPICED PILAF RICE

❖ **SERVES 2** • PREPARATION: 15 MINUTES • COOKING: 20 MINUTES • RESTING: 5 MINUTES ❖

seeds from 3 cardamom pods
pinch of cumin seeds
pinch of coriander seeds

1 tablespoon oil
1 onion, chopped
1 cup basmati rice

1 cinnamon stick
6–7 soft-dried apricots, chopped
salt

1 2
3 4

1	Crush the cardamom, cumin, and coriander seeds using a pestle and mortar (or put them on a chopping board and crush them with the base of a heavy jar).	2	Heat a small saucepan or skillet over a fairly high heat and dry-roast the crushed seeds for about 1 minute, or until the spices release their aroma.	
3	Heat the oil in another pan, add the chopped onion, and cook over a medium heat for 5 minutes.	4	Add the roast spices and stir.	➤

7	Bring to a boil, add a pinch of salt, and stir once.	8	Cover the pan with a lid. If it is not tight-fitting, put a sheet of aluminum foil between the pan and the lid.
5	Add the rice and stir thoroughly with a wooden spoon until all the grains are coated and glistening with oil.	6	Pour in 1½ cups water. Add the cinnamon stick and the chopped apricots.

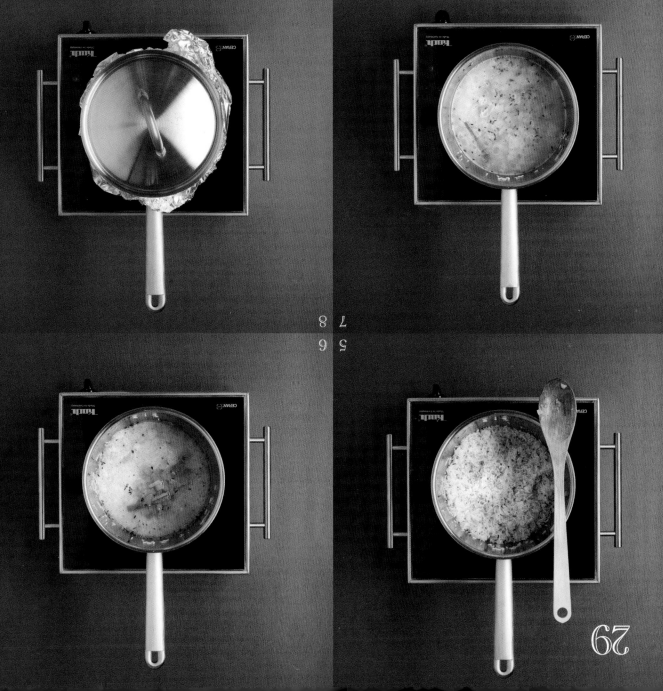

9

Reduce the heat to a minimum and let the pilaf cook for 11 minutes without once lifting the lid. At the end of cooking, remove the pan from the heat, take off the lid, and place a clean kitchen towel over the rice. Let rest for 5 minutes then remove the cinnamon stick. Fork through the rice to fluff it up and serve.

VARIATIONS
❋

For golden rice, add a pinch of saffron threads to the hot water before covering the pan with the lid. For a non-spicy pilaf, simple follow the method omitting the spices and apricots. You can, of course, also leave out the onion.

RISOTTO PRIMAVERA

⊱ SERVES 2 • PREPARATION: 5 MINUTES • COOKING: 30 MINUTES ⊱

4 tablespoons butter
5 oz spring vegetables (such as fava beans, peas, asparagus tips)
1 onion or 2 shallots, chopped

4 cups vegetable or chicken stock
1 cup risotto rice (arborio, carnaroli)
½ glass white wine
1½ oz freshly shredded Parmesan

1 tablespoon crème fraîche or mascarpone (or use an extra tablespoon of butter)
salt and freshly ground pepper

1 2
3 4

1	Melt half the butter in a heavy-based pan or casserole. Add the vegetables and cook them, stirring, over a medium heat for 2 minutes. Remove and set aside.	2	Melt the remaining butter in the pan. Add the onion and cook for 5 minutes over a medium heat. Separately, reheat the stock.
3	Add the rice and stir thoroughly with a wooden spoon until all the grains are coated and glistening with oil.	4	Add the wine and allow to boil until all the liquid is absorbed by the rice. ➤

8	Once the rice is cooked to a creamy perfection, add the Parmesan and mascarpone (or crème fraîche or butter) and beat with the spoon.	7	Add the remaining stock, ladle by ladle, stirring until it is absorbed before adding the next ladleful. This will take 15–20 minutes.
6	Return the vegetables to the pan.	5	Add a ladleful of hot stock and stir until this too has been absorbed.

9	Check the seasoning and adjust if necessary (the stock will already be salted). Serve at once.	**THE RIGHT RICE** ❈ Make sure you choose an Italian-style rice, that is, round-grain.
THE RIGHT TOOL ❈ A wooden spoon with a hole in it is ideal for preparing risotto, allowing you to stir without the rice sticking to the spoon. But you can succeed without it!		**NOTE** ❈ ☛ The amount of stock needed will depend on how quickly the rice absorbs it. Taste as you go and stop when the mixture is creamy but the rice still "al dente."

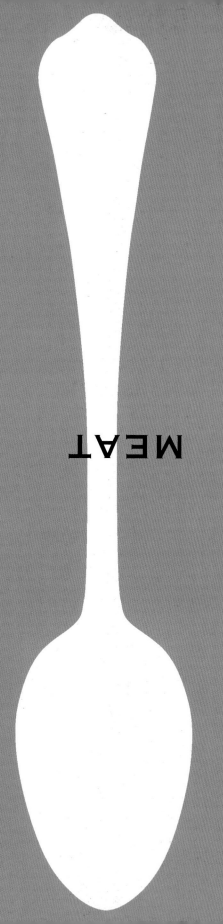

MEAT

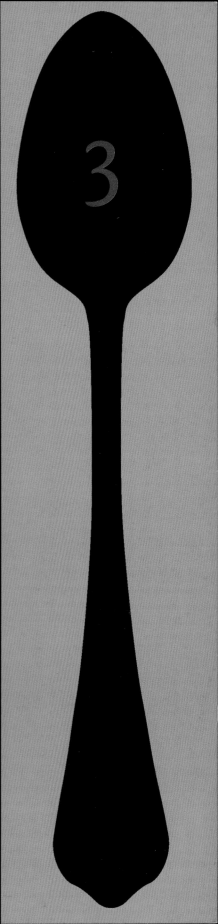

ROASTS

BRAISES

WORLD

ROAST BEEF

❦ **SERVES 6** • **PREPARATION:** 5 MINUTES • **COOKING:** 1 HOUR ❦

2 lb sirloin or rib of beef, rolled and tied
1 small onion, peeled and quartered
2 tablespoons flour

salt and freshly ground pepper
4 cups vegetable stock made with
2 bouillon cubes

IN ADVANCE:
Preheat the oven to 425°F. Select a deep roasting pan that will accommodate the beef comfortably.

1	Put the beef in the roasting pan. Arrange the onion quarters against the sides of the meat. Sprinkle the strip of fat on the beef with a little of the flour, and with salt and pepper.	2	Transfer the pan to the oven. Baste the beef several times with the juices as it cooks.	
3	Cook for 30 minutes for rare meat, 45 minutes for medium.	4	Remove the beef from the oven, place on a board, and cover loosely with aluminum foil to keep hot.	➤

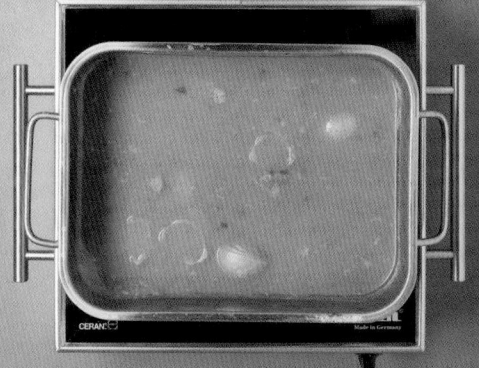

5 6
7 8

5	To make a gravy, place the roasting pan on the hob over a medium heat.	6	Sprinkle the remaining flour into the pan and use a whisk to incorporate the flour.
7	Heat the stock and add a little at a time to the pan, stirring constantly. Bring to a boil then reduce over a gentle heat for about 5 minutes.	8	Taste and season as necessary.

9	Serve the beef with the gravy.

HORSERADISH CREAM
❖

Mix together 2 tablespoons grated horseradish (sold in jars), 1 tablespoon soured cream, ½ teaspoon mustard, salt and freshly ground pepper.

SERVING SUGGESTIONS
❖

Accompany the roast beef with mashed potato or a creamy potato gratin and, in spring, some asparagus stalks drizzled with a little olive oil and roasted in the oven for 20 minutes.

ROAST LAMB

❧ SERVES 6 • PREPARATION: 10 MINUTES • COOKING: 1 HOUR 20 MINUTES ❧

4 lb shoulder or leg of lamb
1 head of garlic
6 thyme stalks + 3 rosemary stalks
2 tablespoons olive oil
salt and pepper

IN ADVANCE:
Preheat the oven to 450°F. Rinse the herbs and remove the leaves from 3 of the thyme stalks and 1 rosemary stalk. Chop the leaves finely.

COOKING TIME:
Depending on the weight of the joint, allow 20 minutes plus 15 minutes for every 1 lb.

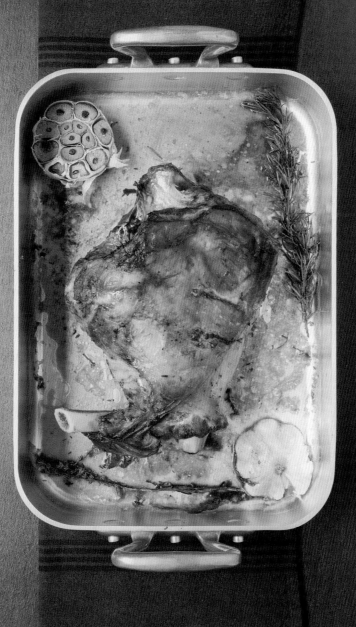

PREPARATION	COOKING
※	※
Put the lamb joint in a large roasting pan. Cut the garlic head in half and add to the pan. Arrange the whole stalks of thyme and rosemary around the meat. Mix the chopped herb leaves with the oil and a little salt and pepper and spread this mixture over the lamb.	Transfer the pan to the oven for 20 minutes, then lower the temperature to 400°F. Cook for 1 hour for slighly pink meat. Remove the lamb from the oven, cover with aluminum foil and let rest for 10 minutes before serving.

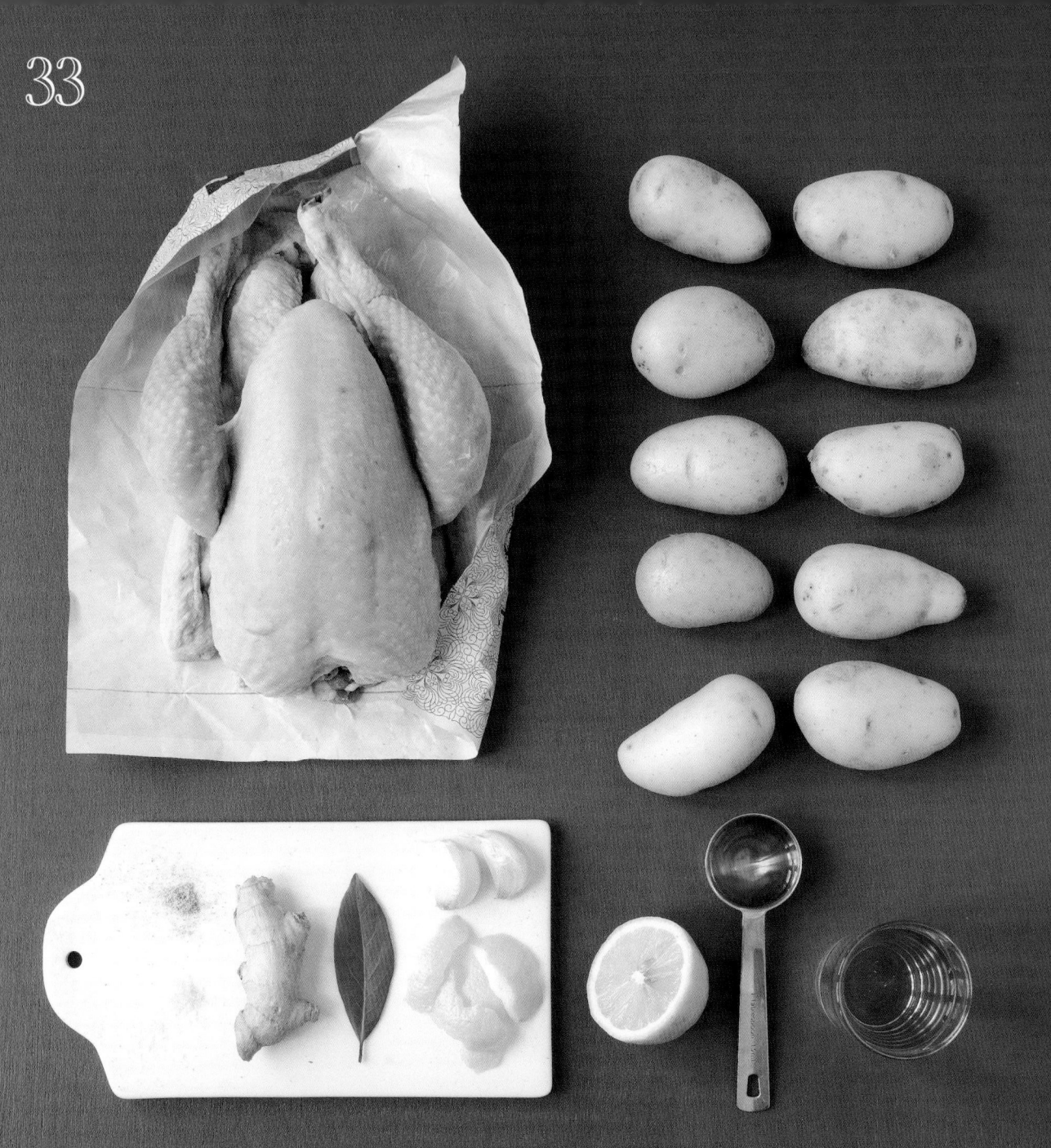

ROAST CHICKEN

✦ **SERVES 4** • PREPARATION: 15 MINUTES • COOKING: 1 HOUR 30 MINUTES ✦

1 good-size roasting chicken (about 3 lb)
1 lemon
1 knob of gingerroot (about 2 inches long)
1 tablespoon olive oil

1–2 garlic cloves
10 medium potatoes
1 glass of white wine

IN ADVANCE:
Preheat the oven to 400°F.

1   Put the chicken in a large, deep-sided roasting pan. Use a paring knife to remove 4–5 wide strips of zest from the lemon. Peel the gingerroot and cut into thin slices. Slip the pared lemon zest and the ginger slices under the skin of the breast of the chicken. Rub the olive oil over the chicken using your hands. Cut the lemon in two, crush the garlic cloves and place them all in the cavity of the chicken. Transfer the roasting pan to the oven.

➤

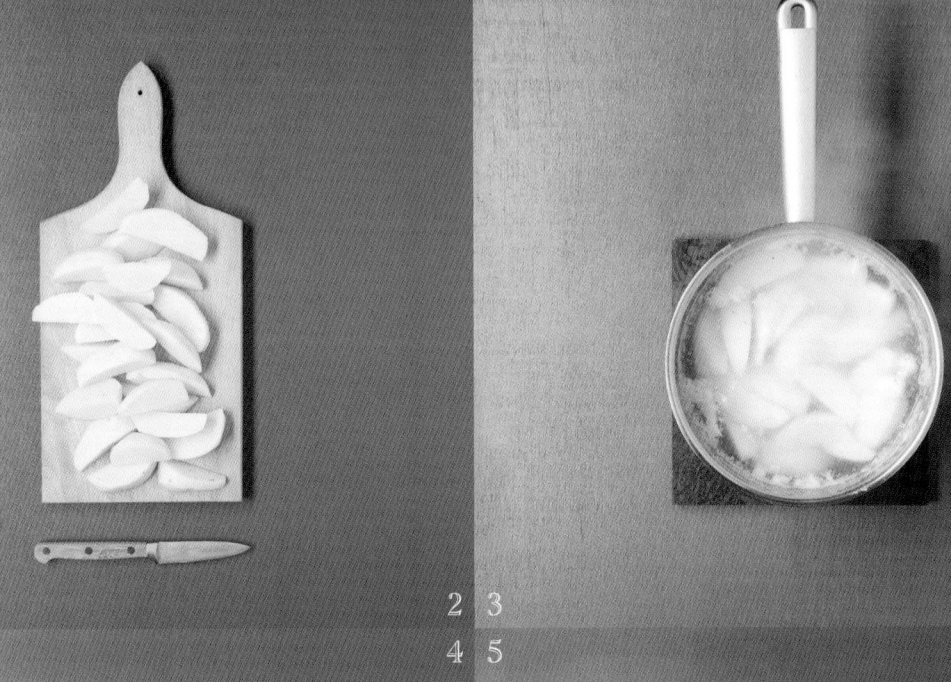

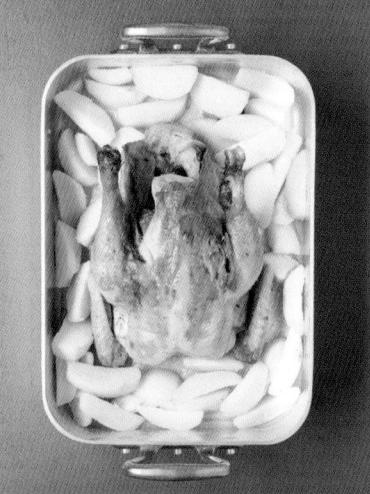

2 | 3
4 | 5

2	Meanwhile peel the potatoes and cut them into large French fries.	3	Cook the potatoes for 10 minutes in a large pan of boiling water. Drain, then shake them a little in the pan.
4	After 45 minutes, turn over the chicken and baste with the juices.	5	Arrange the potatoes around the sides of the roasting pan. They will be crisp and golden at the same time as the chicken.

		TIP ❋	
6	The chicken is cooked when it is golden all over and the thighs come away from the body almost of their own accord.	If you like your breast meat moist, you can begin cooking the chicken upside down: simply place it breast-side down. This way, the fat will run into the breast and make it less dry.	➤

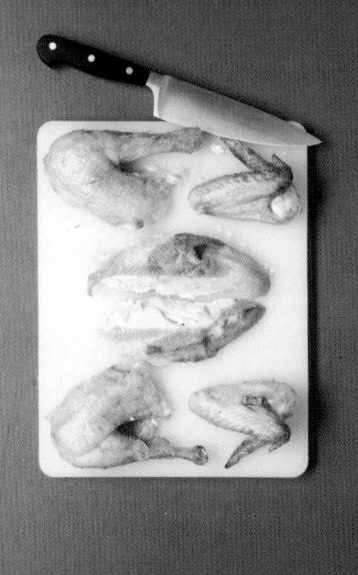

7 8
9 10

7	To carve the bird, transfer to a board and start by removing the thighs with a sharp knife.	8	Next remove the two breasts, then the wings.
9	To make the gravy, remove the potatoes and keep warm. Put the pan on the range. Spoon off the excess fat then add the wine along with the lemon halves and garlic from the bird.	10	Bring to a boil, scraping all the bits from the base of the pan and pressing the garlic and lemon with the back of a wooden spoon. Let it reduce, then discard the garlic and lemon.

11 Serve the chicken with the potatoes and the gravy.

SERVING SUGGESTION
❋

Serve with sliced zucchini, drizzled with olive oil and a little salt then roasted for 20 minutes in a hot oven (400°F).

FURTHER IDEAS
❋

The following day, make a salad with raw shredded vegetables, chopped apple, raisins, and a French dressing enlivened with a pinch of curry powder and some thick yogurt stirred into it. Serve with the leftover chicken.

GUINEAFOWL & STUFFING

❧ SERVES 6 • PREPARATION: 20 MINUTES • COOKING: 2 HOURS ❧

1¼ lb wild mushrooms (such as ceps, girolles), fresh or frozen
3½ oz foie gras
1 chicken breast
6 flat leaf parsley stalks

1 rosemary stalk
2 slices of white bread
scant ½ cup whipping or heavy cream
1 egg
salt and pepper

2 Guineafowl
6 thin smoked bacon slices
2 tablespoons butter

IN ADVANCE:
Preheat the oven to 400°F.

34

1 2
3 4

1	Begin by making the stuffing. Chop 3½ oz of the mushrooms, the foie gras, chicken breast, and the herbs.	2	Soak the bread in the cream. Mix the chopped ingredients with the soaked bread and cream and the egg. Season with salt and pepper.	
3	Place the birds in a large roasting pan and fill the cavities with stuffing. Put the remaining stuffing in the pan alongside the birds.	4	Lay 3 slices of bacon over the breast of each guineafowl.	➤

5 6
7 8

5	Slice the remaining mushrooms.	6	Heat the butter in a skillet over a medium-high heat. Add the mushrooms and brown for 6–7 minutes.
7	Transfer the roasting pan to the oven. Baste the guineafowl midway through cooking.	8	Cook for 1 hour 30 minutes to 2 hours, depending on the weight of your birds: check the label or ask your butcher.

9 Serve the guineafowl with the extra stuffing and mushrooms.

FOR GRAVY
❋

Put the pan on the range over a medium heat, add a glass of white wine (dry or sweet), scrape off the bits from the base, bring to a boil, then reduce.

FOR CHRISTMAS
❋

For a stuffing that is 100 percent Christmas, add 3½ oz chopped chestnuts (sold vacuum sealed). Or, for a traditional English-style Christmas dinner, serve with Brussels sprouts steamed then turned in hot butter and mixed with the whole chestnuts.

BEEF BRAISED IN BEER

❧ **SERVES 4–6** • PREPARATION: 15 MINUTES • COOKING: 3 HOURS ❧

2 lb braising steak, cut into large cubes
2 tablespoons olive oil
6 carrots, peeled and sliced
2 garlic cloves, finely chopped
2 onions cut into rings

1 tablespoon all-purpose flour
2 cups beer
2 thyme stalks
1 bay leaf
salt and freshly ground pepper

IN ADVANCE:
Preheat the oven to 275°F. Prepare all the vegetables.

1	Heat the oil in a Dutch oven over a high heat. Add the beef and brown on both sides.	2	Work in batches: the beef should not be crowded in the pot if it is to brown evenly.	3	Remove the pieces as they brown and set aside in a roasting pan.	
4	Brown the onions in the pot for 4–5 minutes over a medium-high heat.	5	Add the garlic and the carrots and stir everything for 1 minute.	6	Return the meat to the pot.	➤

7 Stir in the flour. Reduce the heat.

NOTE
✳

The flour will thicken the gravy.

VARIATION 1
✳

To make a goulash, add 1 tablespoon of paprika with the flour. Omit the beer and add a large can (14 oz) of chopped tomatoes then, 30 minutes before the cooking time is up, add 1 chopped red bell pepper.

| 8 | Add the beer, the thyme, and the bay leaf and bring gently to a simmer. | **VARIATION 2**
❈
For beef bourguignon, simply use red wine instead of the beer. | ➤ |

| 6 | Cover the pot tightly and transfer to the oven for 2–3 hours. |

❋ LONG AND SLOW

You could leave the pot in the oven for longer at a lower temperature. In this instance, the temperature does not have to be precise.

❋ ON THE RANGE

You can also put the pot on the range but make sure the heat is turned down to a minimum.

10	The meat is cooked when it starts to fall apart. Serve with boiled potatoes and a green salad.

OPTION

—❋—

Add some mushrooms 30 minutes before the end of the cooking time.

TIP

—❋—

This dish is actually better served the following day or the day after. To reheat: put the pot back in a preheated oven at 325°F for 40 minutes or place on the range over a medium heat, bring to a gentle simmer, and heat for 30 minutes.

POT-AU-FEU

❖ **SERVES 4** • **PREPARATION:** 15 MINUTES • **COOKING:** 4 HOURS ❖

2 lb braising steak
3 large or 6 small carrots
4 large leeks, washed and trimmed
1 celery stalk, washed
1 onion, peeled

2 garlic cloves, peeled
3 turnips, peeled
1 small bunch of fresh green herbs
peppercorns and coarsegrain salt
6–10 potatoes, peeled

SUGGESTED CONDIMENTS:
mustard
small dill pickles
tomato sauce

36

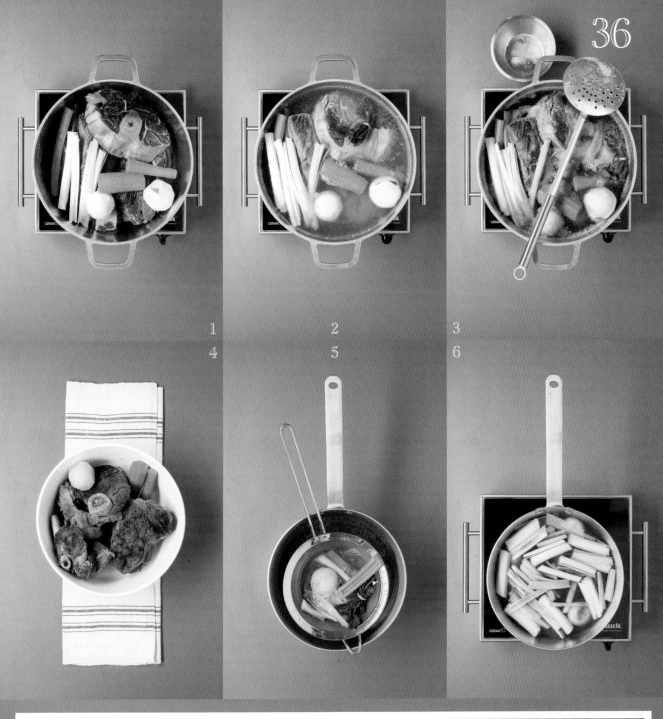

1	Put the meat, 1 carrot, 2 leeks, celery, onion, garlic, 2 turnips, herbs, and peppercorns in a stockpot.	2	Cover with water and bring gently to simmering point.	3	Leave to cook gently bubbling for 3–4 hours, occasionally skimming the foam from the surface.
4	At the end of cooking, lift out the meat and the vegetables.	5	Pour the stock through a strainer into a pan and discard the flavorings.	6	Bring to a boil, then add salt and the remaining vegetables. ➤

7	Cook for 15–20 minutes.	OTHER IDEAS

OTHER IDEAS
❋

Serve the stock just as it is with the vegetables or use as the base for a soup. You could also cook little alphabet pasta in it.

VARIATION
❋

In spring you can vary the vegetables to take advantage of new season peas, fava beans…

8 Serve the stock, the meat, and the vegetables with the condiments.

SALAD FOR THE DAY AFTER
❋

Cut the meat and vegetables into small pieces. Serve with crunchy green salad leaves and chopped dill pickles or with caperberries and tomatoes. Dress with French dressing or the blue cheese version.

COTTAGE PIE
❋

Chop any leftover meat and vegetables as finely as possible and spread in a layer over the base of a gratin dish. Cover with mashed potato, sprinkle with breadcrumbs and put in a preheated oven at 375°F for 20 minutes to brown.

BRAISED VEAL WITH THAI RICE

⇢ SERVES 4 • PREPARATION: 15 MINUTES • COOKING: 1 HOUR 15 MINUTES ⇠

2–2½ lb braising veal, cut into large pieces
1 veal bone if your butcher has one
3 large leeks, trimmed
4–6 carrots

1 onion, peeled and quartered
1 garlic clove
1 oz butter and 1 tablespoon flour
1 vanilla bean

3 fl oz crème fraîche or sour cream
½ lemon
1½ cups Thai rice
salt and pepper

1 2
3 4

1	Put the meat and bone (if using) with 1 leek, 1 carrot, the onion, and garlic in a Dutch oven.	2	Cover with water and bring to a boil. Reduce the heat to a gentle boil and cook, uncovered.
3	After 30 minutes add the remaining vegetables.	4	After 15 minutes, strain the stock into a pan. Set the meat and vegetables to one side. ➤

5	Melt the butter in the pot. Tip in the flour all at once and mix with the butter. Add a ladleful of stock, bring to a boil, stirring with a whisk, then add 3–4 more ladlefuls of the stock.	6	Add the vanilla seeds scraped from the bean and the cream. Cook for 5 minutes over a very low heat then add a squeeze of lemon juice. Taste and adjust the seasoning.
7	Rinse the rice and put in a pan. Pour in 2¼ cups of cold water. Bring to a boil, add salt, and stir.	8	Remove from the heat, cover with a tightly fitting lid and leave for 20 minutes. Remove the lid, and fork through the rice to fluff it up.

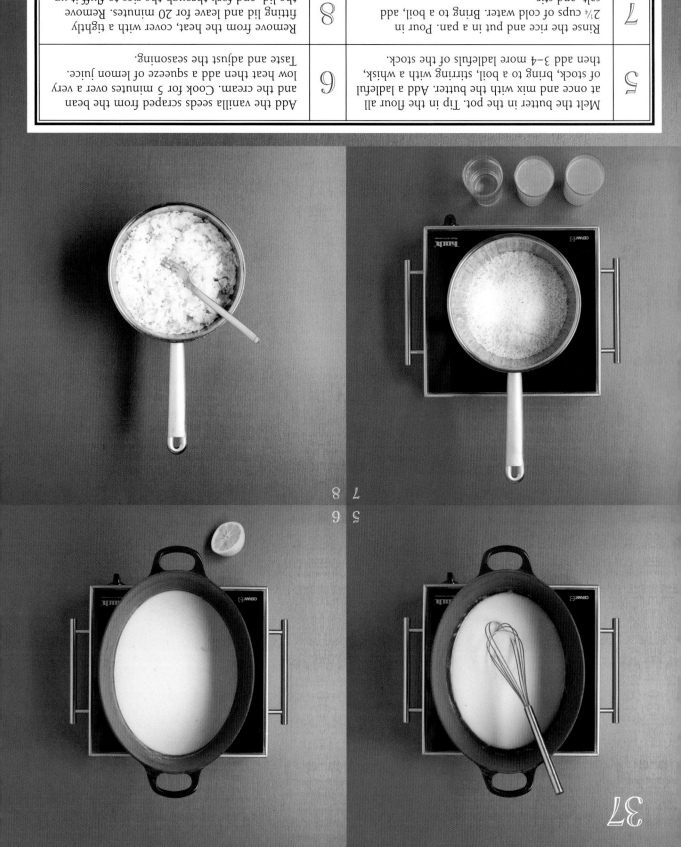

		TIP
9	Return the meat and vegetables to the pot, reheat in the sauce if necessary, then serve with the rice.	You can also cook the rice in the traditional way, for 11 minutes in boiling water, then drain.

RABBIT TAGINE

❧ **SERVES 4 • PREPARATION: 10 MINUTES • COOKING: 1 HOUR 15 MINUTES** ❧

1 rabbit, jointed (ask your butcher to do this)
3 cups prune juice
4 onions, peeled and chopped
2–3 tablespoons olive oil
1 knob of gingerroot (about 2 inches long)

½ teaspoon paprika
1 teaspoon ras-el-hanout
pinch of saffron threads
1 cinnamon stick
salt and freshly ground pepper

12 prunes
6 sun-blush tomatoes (optional)
2 tablespoons honey
6 cilantro stalks
6 flat leaf parsley stalks

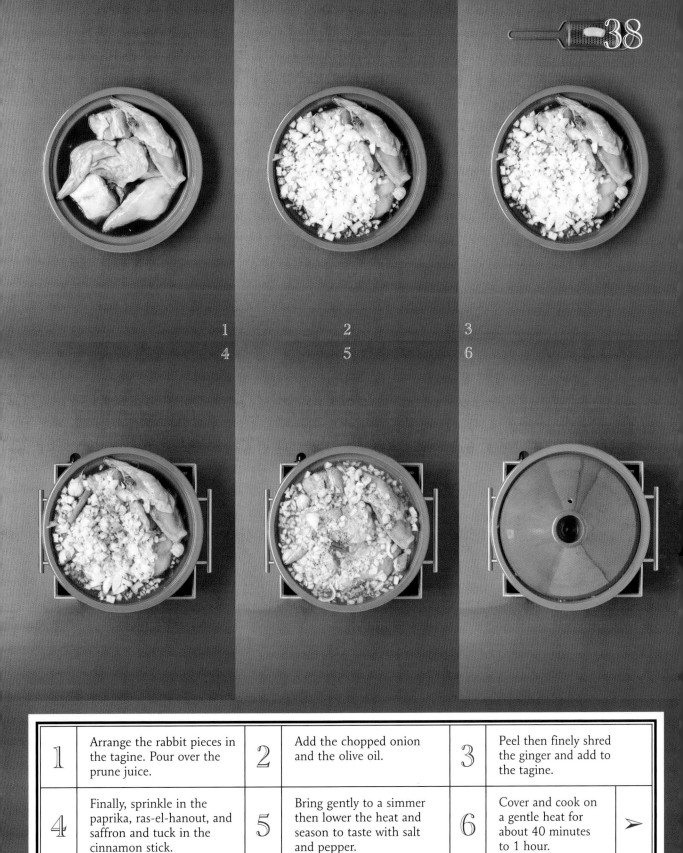

1	Arrange the rabbit pieces in the tagine. Pour over the prune juice.	2	Add the chopped onion and the olive oil.	3	Peel then finely shred the ginger and add to the tagine.
4	Finally, sprinkle in the paprika, ras-el-hanout, and saffron and tuck in the cinnamon stick.	5	Bring gently to a simmer then lower the heat and season to taste with salt and pepper.	6	Cover and cook on a gentle heat for about 40 minutes to 1 hour. ➤

7	Add the prunes and the tomatoes (if using) and continue to cook, covered, for 15 minutes. Lastly, add the honey and cook for a further 10 minutes, uncovered.	**OPTION** ❊ Stir in 1 teaspoonful of orange flower water at the same time as the honey, which gives an even more delectable flavor.

8	Taste and adjust the seasoning if necessary. Serve sprinkled with the chopped herbs.

CARE FOR YOUR TAGINE
❋

Oil the tagine cooking pot before using.

USING THE TAGINE
❋

On electric and ceramic ranges: keep the heat very low. On halogen ranges: inadvisable, unless you have a cast-iron tagine. In the oven: only at a very low temperature (275°F).

CHICKEN, OLIVE, & LEMON TAGINE

VARIATION ON RABBIT TAGINE

Follow the previous recipe for tagine, replacing the rabbit with chicken pieces, the prunes with chopped preserved lemons and 15 olives. Use water instead of prune juice and powdered cumin instead of ras-el-hanout. When you add the preserved lemon, slice 4–5 small zucchini and put them in the tagine to cook for the last 15 minutes.

LAMB & PRUNE TAGINE

VARIATION ON RABBIT TAGINE

❄

Follow the rabbit tagine recipe, replacing the rabbit with 2½ lb lamb fillet, cubed (or leg of lamb steaks) and use water instead of prune juice. To serve, sprinkle with the chopped herbs and 2 tablespoons of sesame seed.

PORK MEATBALLS

❧ **SERVES 4** • PREPARATION: 20 MINUTES • RESTING: 1 HOUR • COOKING: 10 MINUTES ❧

1 large white onion, or 4 scallions
1 garlic clove
6 cilantro stalks
3½ oz pancetta or smoked bacon slices

1 lb ground pork
¼ teaspoon chinese five-spice
salt and freshly ground pepper
2 tablespoons oil

1 2
3 4

1	Put the peeled onion and garlic in the bowl of a food-mixer with the cilantro.	2	Mix until roughly chopped. (You can, of course, also do this by hand using a knife on a wooden board.)	
3	Chop the pancetta or bacon with a sharp cook's knife.	4	Mix everything with the ground pork, then add the spices and salt and pepper. Cover and put in the fridge for 1 hour.	➤

5

Form the mixture into balls no larger than golf balls then flatten them slightly.

VARIATIONS
❊

☛ To make a Thai-flavored version: omit the five-spice and mix in instead the tender hearts of 2 lemongrass stalks, chopped very finely, and 1 small chile, also choppped finely. These meatballs could be served in a rich chicken broth flavored with lemongrass, gingerroot, and lime.

6 Heat the oil in a skillet over a medium-high heat. Brown the meatballs on both sides, allowing about 2 minutes on each side. Reduce the heat and leave to cook for a further 5 minutes. Serve with a little chili pepper sauce, salad, rice, or pita bread.

OPTIONAL SAUCE
❋

☛ When you have cooked the meatballs, wipe out the skillet and return it to the heat. Pour in 1 tablespoon of muscat wine, 2 tablespoons of soy sauce, and 2 tablespoons of dry white wine and stir. Allow to reduce briefly then pour over the meatballs.

CHICKEN TIKKA KABOBS

❖ SERVES 4 • PREPARATION: 20 MINUTES • COOKING: 20 MINUTES • RESTING: MINIMUM 1 HOUR ❖

1 knob of gingerroot
1 garlic clove
2 small pots (4 fl oz size) plain yogurt
½ teaspoon paprika

½–1 teaspoon garam masala
1 tablespoon lemon juice
½ teaspoon olive oil
salt

1 lb chicken (use a mixture of breast and deboned thigh meat), cut into pieces
6 cilantro stalks
½ lemon

1	Peel and shred the gingerroot. Peel and finely chop the garlic. Mix together the ingredients for the marinade: the yogurt, ginger, paprika, garam masala, lemon, oil, and a little salt.

SOURCING SPICES
❋

Garam masala can be bought in Indian stores as well as grocery stores. You could use curry powder.

HOMEMADE GARAM MASALA
❋

Heat a skillet until hot then dry-roast 3 tablespoons coriander seeds, 2 tablespoons cumin seeds, the seeds from 5 cardamom pods, 5 cloves, 1 cinnamon stick, ½ tablespoon black peppercorns, 1 bay leaf, and ¼ teaspoon ground nutmeg. Once they give off their aroma, tip into a mortar and grind to a powder.

➤

2

Place the chicken pieces in the marinade, stir to coat, and leave to marinate for 1 hour (and up to 1 day) in the fridge.

❋
MARINATING TIME

This dish is not quite so good if you do not have time to marinate the chicken. The yogurt tenderizes the meat and the spices flavor it.

3	Preheat the broiler or prepare a grill. Thread the chicken pieces onto metal skewers. Broil them for about 10 minutes on each side until they are golden brown all over.	**COOKING** ❋ The kabobs are delicious cooked on a grill but wait until the flames have died down, otherwise you risk burning the marinade covering the chicken.
	SERVING SUGGESTION ❋ Enjoy the kabobs sprinkled with chopped cilantro and a squeeze of lemon served with naan or pita bread.	**ANOTHER IDEA** ❋ These kabobs are also good served cold, for a picnic, perhaps.

LIGHT MOUSSAKA

❖ SERVES 4 • PREPARATION: 25 MINUTES • COOKING: 1 HOUR 10 MINUTES ❖

2 large or 3 small eggplants
6–8 tablespoons olive oil
2 large lamb leg steaks, cut into pieces
3–4 tomatoes

6 flat leaf parsley stalks, leaves washed and
stripped
2–3 slices of day-old bread for bread crumbs
salt and pepper

¼ teaspoon powdered cinnamon
1½ cups Béchamel Sauce (see recipe 06)

IN ADVANCE:
Preheat the oven to 425°F.

1	Wash the eggplants and cut them into slices about ¼-inch thick.	2	Spread them out in a single layer on a baking sheet and brush them with 3 tablespoons of olive oil.	3	Roast the eggplant slices for 20–30 minutes. You may need to cook them in two batches.
4	Heat 1 tablespoon oil in a heavy skillet. Cook the lamb over a medium heat.	5	Chop the cooked lamb into small pieces. Slice the tomatoes.	6	Chop the parsley, mix with the bread crumbs, and season. ➤

7	Oil a large pan. Build up layers of eggplant, meat, tomatoes, and seasoning. Cover with béchamel and bread crumbs and sprinkle with oil.

IMPORTANT

☞ Between each layer you need to season with salt, pepper, and cinnamon, for that true Greek flavor.

OPTION 1

※ If liked, add a layer of soft sheep's cheese (or Greek yogurt). For a vegetarian option, it can replace the meat.

OPTION 2

※ You can of course use ready-prepared ground lamb, or beef, or veal, for a less pronounced flavor.

43

8	Transfer to the oven and cook for 30 minutes. Serve with a green salad.

NOTE
❋

☛ This modern take on the classic recipe for moussaka is neither too light nor too heavy.

OPTION 3
❋

For a more authentic version use ready-prepared ground lamb, a good layer of tomato sauce, and even a layer of boiled potatoes, cut into slices.

FISH & SHELLFISH

CLASSICS

PAN-FRIED

MARINATED

4

FISH PARCELS WITH 3 SAUCES

❦ SERVES 4 • PREPARATION: 5 MINUTES • COOKING: 15 MINUTES ❦

4 salmon steaks, about 5 oz each
1 tablespoon olive oil
1 lemon, salt, and freshly ground pepper

IN ADVANCE:
Preheat the oven to 400°F.

HOW TO COOK IN PARCELS:
Place the salmon steaks on a large sheet of aluminum foil brushed with olive oil. Season with salt, pepper, and a squeeze of lemon juice.

Wrap the steaks to completely seal but do not enclose them tightly: the hot air needs to circulate inside the parcel as they cook. Fold over all edges to seal the foil. Cook for 10–15 minutes.

1 2
3 4

GREEN SAUCE ❋		YOGURT SAUCE ❋	
1 & 2	Roughly blend in a food-mixer: ½ bunch flat leaf parsley, 1 small red onion or 2 spring onions, 2 tarragon sprigs, 1 tablespoon capers, 2 tablespoons olive oil, and 2 teaspoons wholegrain mustard.	3	Mix together 6 finely chopped dill fronds with 2 individual pots Greek-style yogurt and 1 tablespoon lemon juice.
		PEA & BASIL SAUCE ❋	
		4	Blend together 2 cups cooked peas with 6 basil stalks and 1 tablespoon olive oil.

STEAMED VEGETABLES & FISH

❖ **SERVES 2** • PREPARATION: 10 MINUTES • COOKING: 20 MINUTES ❖

2 small whole fish (sea bass or sea bream, for example)
1 knob of gingerroot, about 1½–2 inches long

selection of spring vegetables
2 tablespoons oil
3 tablespoons soy sauce
pinch of sugar

IN ADVANCE:
Make diagonal cuts on both sides of the fish, through to the bone. Peel the ginger, cut half into fine slices, and shred the rest.

1	Place the fish in a steamer with the slices of gingerroot on top. Peel and cut the vegetables into short lengths and place them inside the steamer with the fish.	2	Steam for 12–15 minutes according to the thickness of the fish: once cooked, the flesh should flake easily.
3	Heat the oil in a small skillet or pan. Add the shredded ginger and stir around for 1 minute.	4	Off the heat, add the soy sauce and the sugar. Pour over the fish and vegetables and serve.

BREADED FISH FILLETS

➔ **SERVES 2** • PREPARATION: 20 MINUTES • COOKING: 10 MINUTES ➔

2 slices dry bread
peel and juice of 1 lemon
1 bunch of herbs or a mixture, leaves
stripped and washed

salt
2 tablespoons butter
2 fish fillets, not too thick (salmon,
trout, sole…)

IN ADVANCE:
Preheat the oven to 400°F.

1	Use a food-mixer to reduce the bread to crumbs.	2	Add the lemon peel and the herbs and quickly reduce to a powder. Season with salt.	3	Melt the butter in a small pan and add the lemon juice.
4	Press the fish fillets in the bread-crumb mixture to coat both sides then transfer to a baking dish.	5	Sprinkle over the remaining bread crumbs then pour the melted butter on top.	6	Cook for 6–10 minutes according to the thickness of the fillets. Serve with a little green salad.

MUSSELS WITH TARRAGON

➤ **SERVES 2** • PREPARATION: 10 MINUTES • COOKING: 10 MINUTES ❖

4 pints mussels, cleaned
2 tablespoons butter
2–3 shallots or 1 onion
1 glass of white wine

1 good long tarragon stalk with plenty of leaves

IN ADVANCE:
Clean the mussels in cold water with a small brush or knife. Discard any broken ones or those that remain open.

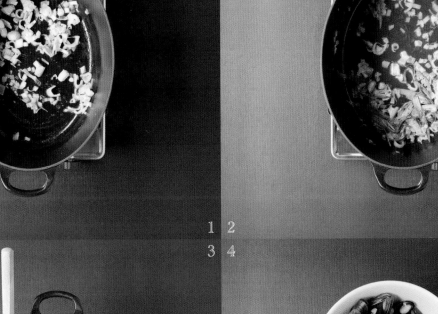

1	Melt the butter in a Dutch oven. Finely chop the shallots. Cook gently in the butter for 5 minutes over a medium heat.	2	Increase the heat to high, then add the white wine and the tarragon.
3	Add the mussels, cover the pan tightly with the lid, and cook for 3–5 minutes, shaking the pan from time to time.	4	Serve immediately—French fries are a traditional accompaniment.

SCALLOPS WITH GARLIC & GINGER

SERVES 2 • **PREPARATION: 10 MINUTES** • **COOKING: 10 MINUTES**

8–10 prepared scallops off the shell
(or use frozen ones and defrost)
1 garlic clove and/or a small piece
of gingerroot

6 fresh flat leaf parsley or cilantro stalks
4 tablespoons butter

IN ADVANCE:
Defrost the scallops if using frozen.
Spread them out on a dish and leave in the
fridge for 4 hours.

1	Finely chop the garlic. Wash and dry the herbs, strip the leaves, and chop finely.	2	Melt half the butter in a skillet over a medium-high heat until it foams.	3	Add the scallops and cook for 2–3 minutes on one side.
4	Turn the scallops over and cook for 1–2 minutes on the second side. Remove to a plate. Discard the butter.	5	Melt the remaining butter until it foams. Add in the garlic, stir for 1 minute, then add the herbs.	6	Pour the garlic and herb butter over the scallops and serve immediately.

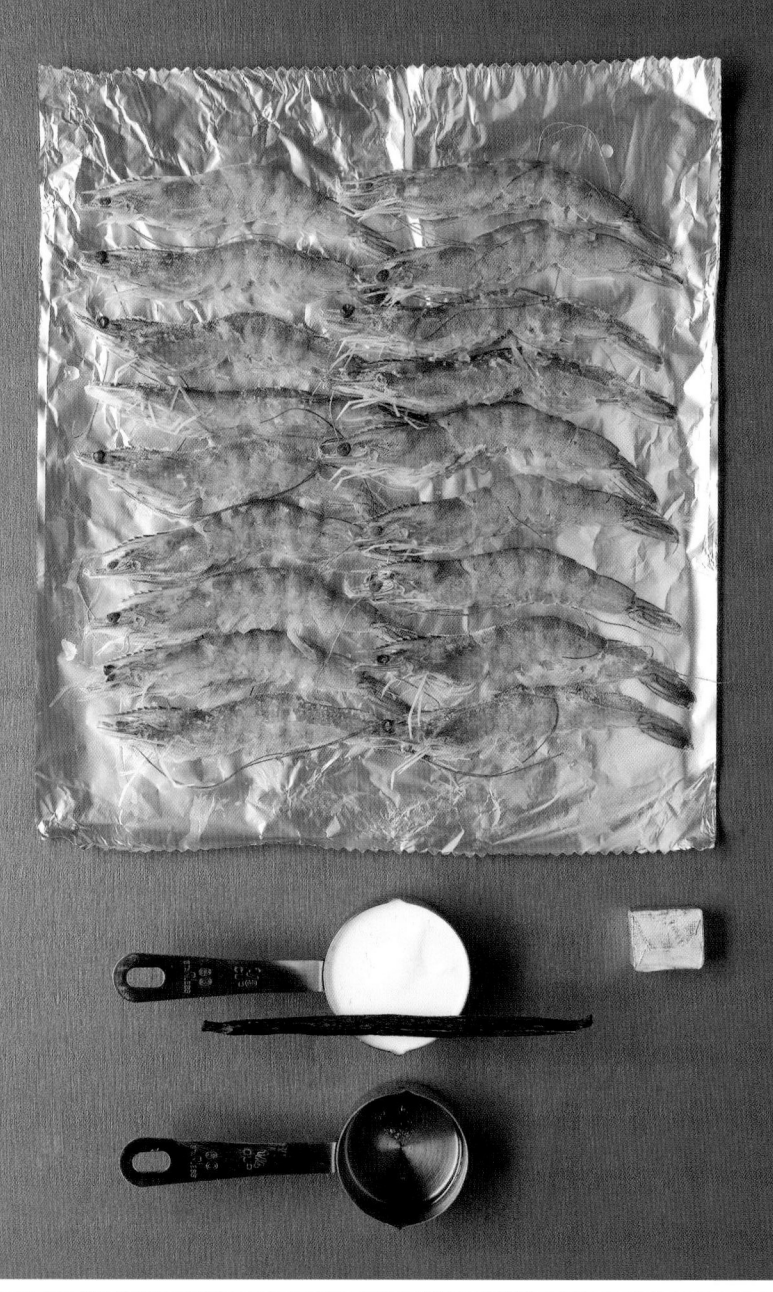

JUMBO SHRIMP & VANILLA SAUCE

❧ SERVES 4 • PREPARATION: 10 MINUTES • COOKING: 10 MINUTES ❧

VANILLA SAUCE:
1 cup vegetable or fish stock
5 tablespoons light or whipping cream
1 vanilla bean, split in two

2 tablespoons olive oil
16–20 whole jumbo shrimp, unshelled

1 2
3 4

1	First make the sauce. Pour the stock and the cream into a small pan. Scrape the vanilla seeds into the pan and put in the bean too. Heat gently together.	2	Heat the olive oil in a large ridged skillet and fry the jumbo shrimp on one side for 2–3 minutes. Do not overcrowd the pan; work in batches if necessary.
3	Turn over the shrimp and cook on the second side for 2 minutes.	4	Serve the shrimp with the sauce.

JUST-COOKED TUNA STEAK

⇢ SERVES 2 • COOKING: 1 MINUTE ⇠

1 tablespoon olive oil
1 large (or 2 small) tuna steaks
either: soy sauce, wasabi, pickled
ginger (sushi ginger)

or: 1 tablespoon wholegrain mustard
salt

1 2
3 4

1	Heat the oil in a skillet. Seal the tuna for just 30 seconds on one side.	2	Turn over the tuna and cook the second side for another 30 seconds.
3	Serve with Japanese condiments.	4	Alternatively, serve with wholegrain mustard and a little salt.

CEVICHE WITH LIME

❖ **SERVES 2** • PREPARATION: 15 MINUTES • CHILLING: 30 MINUTES ❖

2 fillets of sea bass prepared by your
fishmonger (the fish must be ultra-fresh)
4 tablespoons olive oil
1–2 limes

juice of 1 orange
1 fennel bulb
salt and pepper

1 2
3 4

1	Remove any bones from the fish fillets using your fingers or fish tweezers then cut the fillets into strips.	2	Put the fish into a nonmetallic dish and pour over the oil.
3	Pare the peel of the limes and squeeze the juice. Mix with the orange juice. Wash and trim the fennel bulb then cut into fine slices.	4	Pour the juice and peel over the fish and add the fennel slices. Season with salt and pepper. Serve immediately or within a maximum of 30 minutes if you prefer the fish more "cooked."

TUNA TAHITIAN-STYLE

❊ **SERVES 4** • **PREPARATION:** 15 MINUTES • CHILLING: 30 MINUTES ❊

4 small boneless tuna fillets
(ask your fishmonger to bone them for you)
½ cucumber
2–3 limes

1 cup coconut milk
1 tablespoon olive oil
salt and freshly ground pepper
¼ bunch of cilantro

1	Cut the tuna into small cubes. Peel, deseed, and shred the cucumber.	2	Pare the peel of 1 lime and squeeze the juice from 4 lime halves.
3	Mix together the ingredients for the marinade in a nonmetallic dish: the cucumber, lime peel and juice, coconut milk, and olive oil. Season with salt and pepper.	4	Put the tuna in the dish and sprinkle with chopped cilantro. Serve immediately or within a maximum of 30 minutes if you prefer the tuna more "cooked" in the lime juice.

VEGETABLES

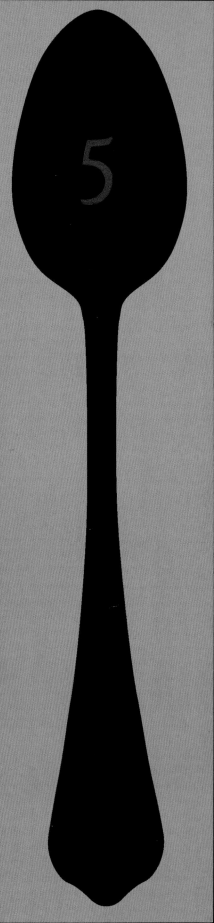

SOUPS & CO.

BAKED VEGETABLES

ONE-POT VEGETABLES

RAW & SIMPLY COOKED

SQUASH SOUP

❖ **SERVES 4** • PREPARATION: 25 MINUTES • COOKING: 1 HOUR ❖

1 Hokkaido squash or other variety
1 slice of pumpkin
3 potatoes
2 vegetable or chicken bouillon cubes

salt and freshly ground pepper
6 chervil stalks
4 tablespoons crème fraîche, sour cream,
or coconut milk

IN ADVANCE:
Preheat the oven to 400°F.

1 2
3 4

1	Put the squash and the pumpkin, unpeeled, in an ovenproof dish. Roast for 30–40 minutes: the flesh should give when tested with a knife.	2	Remove the vegetables from the oven. Cut the squash in half, remove and discard the seeds and fibers. Scoop the flesh from the skins.
3	While the squash and pumpkin are roasting, peel the potatoes, cut into pieces, and place in a large pan. Cover them with water then add the bouillon cubes.	4	Bring to a boil and cook the potatoes for 20–25 minutes or until they are tender when tested with a knife. ➢

5

Put the squash and pumpkin flesh into the pan with the potatoes. Mix with a stick-blender (or transfer everything to an electric blender, or pass through a food mill) until smooth and evenly blended. Check the seasoning and add salt and pepper if necessary. Chop the chervil.

❋ IF YOUR SOUP IS TOO THICK...

Stir in a little water, milk, or extra stock.

❋ OPTION

Squash and pumpkin go very well with gingerroot. If you wish, finely shred a small piece of gingerroot and add before you blend the soup.

6	Serve the soup with a spoonful of cream or coconut milk in each bowl, and sprinkled with the chopped chervil.	**DE-LUXE VERSION** ※ In place of the cream, top each bowl with shavings of foie gras before serving.
TIPS ※		**FOR A MEAL IN ITSELF** ※
You can use other varieties of squash, such as butternut, to make this soup. The potatoes help to thicken it, while offsetting the sweetness of the pumpkin.		Add some cubes of cheese, croûtons, or cooked smoked bacon, cut into cubes.

NEW STYLE GAZPACHO

➤ **SERVES 4** • **PREPARATION: 25 MINUTES** • **COOKING: 15 MINUTES** ◄

6–8 tomatoes
1 cucumber
2 red bell peppers
1 red onion

1 very small melon or ¼ watermelon
1 avocado
3 tablespoons olive oil
6 slices country-style bread

1–3 small garlic cloves, according to taste,
finely chopped
salt and freshly ground pepper
Tabasco sauce

1

Skin the tomatoes by dropping them for 1–2 minutes into boiling water; the skins then slip off easily. Cut each one in half and remove the seeds. Peel and deseed the cucumber and deseed the bell peppers. Peel and chop the onion. Cut the melon or watermelon, removing all seeds and the skins.

Cut the following into tiny dice: 1 tomato, quarter of the cucumber, 1 slice of melon, 1 avocado, quarter of the onion, and quarter of the bell pepper. Reserve as garnish. Cut the remaining vegetables and the melon into large pieces.

2	Put the roughly chopped vegetables and melon into a food-mixer with 2 tablespoons olive oil and 2 slices of bread, crusts removed.	3	Whiz everything until smooth. Season to taste with salt, pepper, and Tabasco sauce.
4	Cover with plastic wrap and leave in a cool place for several hours.	5	For the croûtons: preheat the oven to 400°F. Cut the bread into cubes, spread on a cookie sheet, scatter over the garlic, and drizzle with oil. Cook for 10–15 minutes.

6	Serve the soup well chilled with ice cubes and the reserved vegetables in each bowl. Hand round the croûtons separately.	**OTHER FRUIT IDEAS** ❋ Use ripe mango in place of the melon.
TIP ❋	☛ The gazpacho is best if it can be chilled for several hours in the fridge before serving.	**VARIATION** ❋ You can add a large glass of cultured buttermilk, if you wish.

SPRING MINESTRONE

❖ SERVES 6 • PREPARATION: 35 MINUTES • COOKING: 3 HOURS 30 MINUTES • SOAKING: OVERNIGHT ❖

2 oz Parmesan + 1 rind of Parmesan
leaves from 4 basil stalks, torn into pieces
salt and freshly ground pepper
3½ oz short-length pasta

1 onion + 2 garlic cloves
4–6 tablespoons olive oil
8 oz cherry tomatoes
3 chicken or vegetable bouillon cubes
dissolved in 6 cups water

¼ spring cabbage
2 small zucchini
1 fennel bulb
3 potatoes
⅔ cup navy beans (dried or canned)

1	If using dried navy beans, put them in cold water to soak overnight.	2	The following day, put the beans in a pan with fresh water and cook, uncovered, for 30–40 minutes.	3	Dice the potatoes, fennel, and zucchini and slice the cabbage. Finely chop the onion and garlic.
4	Heat the oil in a pan. Cook the onion and garlic, then the potatoes, for 2–3 minutes.	5	Add the fennel and cabbage next, and cook for a further 2–3 minutes.	6	Add three-quarters of the tomatoes and the zucchini. ➤

7 8
9 10

7	Pour in the stock and then add in the rind of Parmesan and the torn basil leaves. Bring to a boil then reduce the heat to low.	8	Let cook for 2 hours, covered, stirring occasionally to prevent it sticking.
9	Taste and adjust the seasoning if necessary. Add the pasta and the reserved zucchni and tomatoes.	10	Add the cooked beans (or the canned ones, if using) and continue to cook for a further 20 minutes.

11	Serve with Parmesan shavings, pesto, and good-quality bread.	**RUSTIC FLAVOR** Minestrone is even better if you add a ham bone with the stock in step 7.
OTHER IDEAS FOR SPRING MINESTRONE Use fava beans, peas, or green beans.		**TIP** Minestrone is a meal in itself. Follow it with just a light dessert: a citrus fruit salad or strawberries in season.

RED LENTIL DAHL

❧ SERVES 4 • PREPARATION: 15 MINUTES • COOKING: 25 MINUTES ❧

8 oz split red lentils
1 onion
1 small can of tomatoes

1 cinnamon stick
6 green cardamom pods
¼ teaspoon cumin seeds

couple of pinches of turmeric
½ cup coconut milk
1 lime

1	Rinse the lentils thoroughly in a colander.	2	Put the lentils in a large pan with the roughly chopped onion, the tomatoes, and the spices.
3	Add 2 cups of water. Bring to the boil and cook, uncovered, for about 25 minutes until the lentils start to lose their shape.	4	Remove and discard the cinnamon stick and the cardamom pods. ➤

| 5 | Blend the lentils in a food-mixer until smooth. |

✳ FOR A MORE PRONOUNCED FLAVOR

Return the seeds from 1–2 cardamom pods to the lentils just before blending.

✳ IF YOU DON'T HAVE A FOOD-MIXER

You can serve the dahl unblended, in which case you need to chop the onion and the tomatoes finely before adding them to the pan.

6	Return the dahl to the pan over a gentle heat, then add in the coconut milk and a squeeze of lime juice. Serve immediately.

OPTION
❈

Instead of the coconut milk you can use Greek-style yogurt.

VARIATIONS
❈

You can make this into a soup by using twice the amount of water for cooking the lentils. Alternatively, you can use less water to cook the lentils then dry them out further in a skillet with a little oil and ½ teaspoon of garam masala. Serve as a dip.

MASHED POTATO

❧ **SERVES 4** • **PREPARATION:** 20 MINUTES • **COOKING:** 30 MINUTES ❧

ESSENTIAL:
Do not be tempted to use a food-mixer, the resultant mash will be far too elastic.

IN ADVANCE:
Wash the potatoes.

2 lb floury potatoes
salt
4 tablespoons butter
3 tablespoons crème fraîche or sour cream
6 tablespoons milk

1	Put the potatoes in a large pan. Cover with cold water, add a little salt, and bring to a boil.	2	Allow the potatoes to boil gently with the pan half-covered, for 20–30 minutes, depending on their size.	3	Drain then peel the potatoes. Return them to the pan and allow to dry for a few seconds over the heat.
4	Add the butter and the cream and mash in using a potato creamer.	5	Heat the milk and then beat into the mash using a wooden spoon.	6	Check the seasoning, add salt if necessary, and serve immediately.

OVEN-BAKED RATATOUILLE

❖ SERVES 6 • PREPARATION: 25 MINUTES • COOKING: 40 MINUTES ❖

3 large or 6 smaller tomatoes
3 zucchini
2 small eggplants
1–2 red or yellow bell peppers
1–2 red onions and 1 garlic clove

2 basil stalks
½ teaspoon sugar
1 teaspoon vinegar
2 tablespoons olive oil
salt and freshly ground pepper

IN ADVANCE:
Preheat the oven to 400°F.

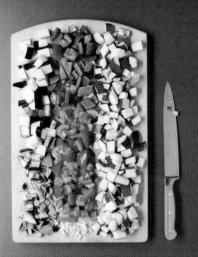

1 2
3 4

1	Wash all the vegetables then cut them into small cubes.	2	Put everything in a shallow-sided baking dish or on a cookie tray. Pour in the oil and mix in carefully. Season with salt and pepper.
3	Transfer to the oven and cook for 40 minutes.	4	Add the vinegar mixed with the sugar and sprinkle with chopped basil. Serve hot or cold.

ROASTED ROOT VEGETABLES

➤ **SERVES 6** • PREPARATION: 25 MINUTES • COOKING: 1 HOUR ➤

3 lb mixed root vegetables (carrots, potatoes, parsnips, sunchokes, turnips, celeriac, rutabagas…)
3 tablespoons olive oil

4 thyme stalks
4 chervil stalks
4 tablespoons mascarpone or heavy cream
salt and freshly ground pepper

IN ADVANCE:
Preheat the oven to 375°F.

1 2
3 4

1	Wash and peel all the vegetables and cut them uniformly into large fries.	2	Spread them out on a cookie tray, drizzle with oil, tuck in the thyme, and mix well.
3	Transfer to the oven and roast for 1 hour.	4	Chop the chervil and mix with the mascarpone, season with salt and pepper, and serve over the hot roasted vegetables.

STUFFED VEGETABLES

➤ **SERVES 4** • PREPARATION: 30 MINUTES • COOKING: 1 HOUR 20 MINUTES ➤

4 medium tomatoes
3 zucchini
2 red bell peppers
3 onions
3 tablespoons olive oil

3–4 scallions
1–2 garlic cloves
6 basil sprigs
3½ oz ground veal
1½ oz Parmesan

1 egg
2 tablespoons bread crumbs
salt and pepper
IN ADVANCE:
Preheat the oven to 400°F.

1 2
3 4

1	Wash all the vegetables. Slice the tops off the tomatoes and use a teaspoon to remove the seeds, juice, and centers. Reserve.	2	Split the zucchini down their length, then remove the seeds and core, keeping about ¼ inch of flesh on all sides. Reserve.
3	Cut 1 bell pepper lengthways and remove the seeds and membranes.	4	Core the onions and reserve the centers. ➤

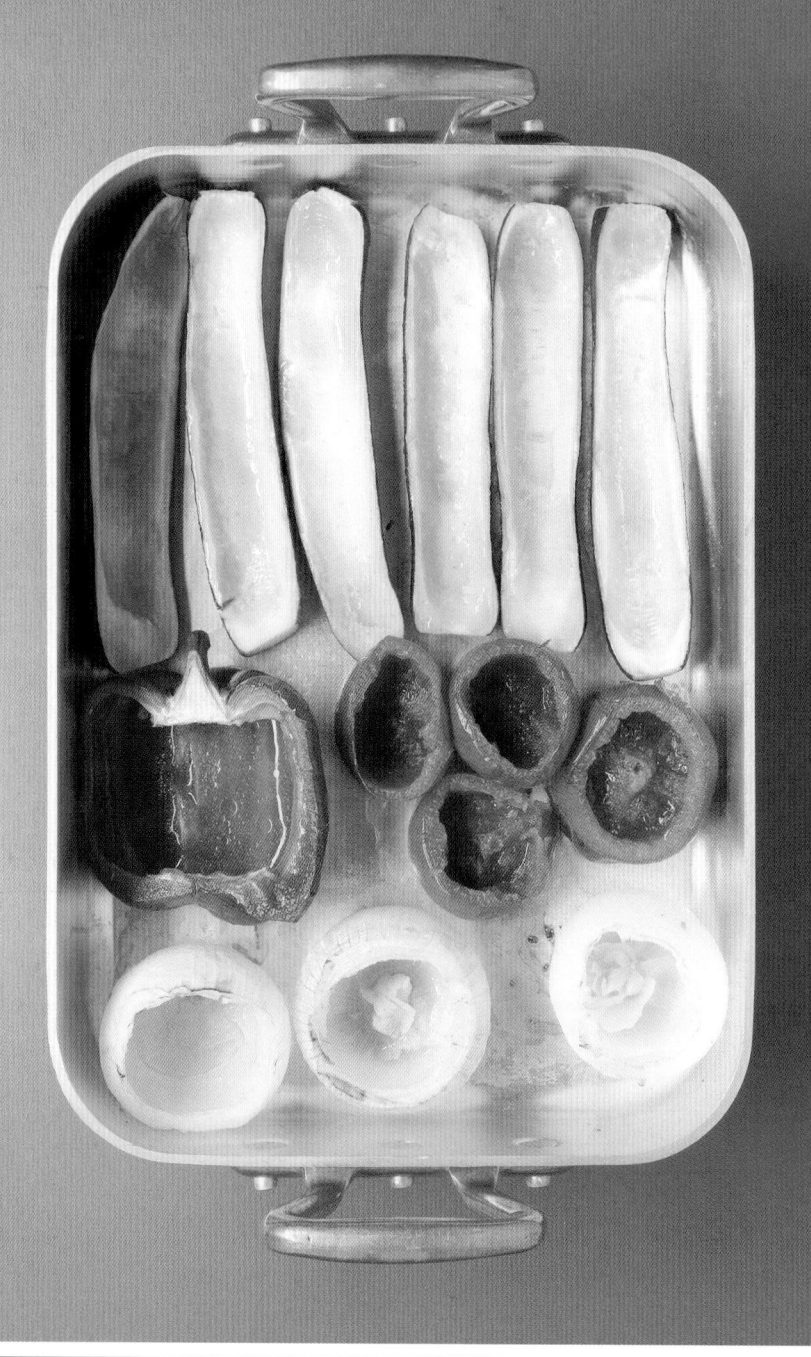

5	Put all the prepared vegetables in a baking pan and drizzle with 1 tablespoon of the oil. Transfer to the oven and cook for 20 minutes.	**TIP** ☞ Use a pastry brush to make the task of oiling the cored vegetables easier.
OPTION	If you can find them, use round zucchini; they are practical to stuff and look attractive.	**TIP** You may wish to cook the onion and bell pepper for a further 15–20 minutes: they will be softer and less crunchy.

6 7
8 9

FOR THE STUFFING

6	Chop the reserved vegetable flesh using a food-mixer or by hand.	7	Finely chop the scallions, the remaining bell pepper, the garlic, and basil.	
8	Heat the oil in a skillet and cook the onions for 5 minutes then add the chopped bell pepper and cook for a further 5 minutes.	9	Add the chopped vegetables to the pan. Cook, stirring, for 5 minutes.	➤

10 Add the meat to the skillet and cook until it is lightly browned. Add the grated Parmesan and the egg. Sprinkle in the bread crumbs and season with salt and pepper.

❋ OPTION

Veal makes a light stuffing but you can just as well use ground pork or lamb.

❋ VEGETARIAN STUFFING

Instead of using meat, use the chopped flesh of an extra 2 tomatoes, 2 zucchini, and 2 bell peppers and add in a handful of different chopped herbs to give the dish even more flavor.

11	Fill the prepared vegetables with the stuffing and transfer to the oven for 45 minutes.

SERVING SUGGESTION
❈

Serve with Camargue or risotto rice.

SOFT CHEESE STUFFING
❈

Mix 2 cups of ricotta, soft sheep's cheese, or cottage cheese, ¼ teaspoon harissa paste, and ½ bunch of chopped flat leaf parsley. Stuff the prepared vegetables as before and cook in the oven for a further 20 minutes.

ZUCCHINI CRUMBLE

❧ SERVES 4 • PREPARATION: 25 MINUTES • COOKING: 45 MINUTES ❧

4 tablespoons whole almonds

2 lb zucchini, washed and trimmed

salt and freshly ground pepper

2 tablespoons olive oil

5 tablespoons butter

scant cup wholewheat flour

¼ teaspoon sugar

¼ teaspoon vinegar

1 cup cottage or quark cheese

leaves from 6 basil stalks, chopped

IN ADVANCE:

Preheat the oven to 425°F. Roughly chop the almonds.

| 1 | Coarsely shred the zucchini. Season with salt and pepper and drizzle with 1 tablespoon of olive oil. | 2 | Transfer to a gratin dish and cook at the top of the oven for 15 minutes. | 3 | Use your fingertips to rub the butter into the flour. Add the remaining oil and the almonds. Season with salt. |
| 4 | Mix the sugar and vinegar with the zucchini, then the cottage cheese and basil. | 5 | Spread the crumble over the dish. Set the oven to 350°F. | 6 | Transfer the crumble to the oven. Bake for 25 minutes to brown the top. Serve. |

CREAMY POTATO GRATIN

❖ **SERVES 6** • PREPARATION: 20 MINUTES • COOKING: 1 HOUR 30 MINUTES ❖

2 lb waxy potatoes
1 garlic clove
2 tablespoons butter

salt and freshly ground pepper
2½ cups heavy cream

IN ADVANCE:
Preheat the oven to 325°F.

1	Peel the potatoes and cut into very thin (⅛-inch) slices, either by hand or using a food-mixer.	2	Cut the garlic clove in half and rub them over the sides and base of a large gratin dish. Butter the dish generously.
3	Put the sliced potatoes in the dish and season with salt and pepper. Pour in the cream to cover.	4	Transfer to the oven for 1¼–1½ hours, by which time the top should be crisp and golden, the potatoes cooked, and the cream reduced.

10 onions

3 tablespoons oil or 3 tablespoons butter

7 oz good-quality ready-rolled puff pastry (preferably all-butter)

½ teaspoon dried oregano

4–8 anchovies in oil (optional)

IN ADVANCE:

Preheat the oven to 425°F. Cut the anchovies (if using) into thin fillets.

63

1 2
3 4

1	Peel and halve the onions then cut them into slices, not too thinly.	2	Heat the oil or butter in a pan with the onions. Soften for 30–35 minutes over a very gentle heat.
3	Unroll the pastry onto a cookie sheet and prick with a fork. Mark a ½-inch border. Spread the cooked onions up to the border and sprinkle with oregano. Top with anchovies.	4	Cook in the oven for about 20 minutes or until the pastry is golden brown. Serve with a green salad.

VEGETABLE HOT-POT

❧ SERVES 6 • PREPARATION: 20 MINUTES • COOKING: 15 MINUTES ❧

8 small young carrots or 4 large ones
8 small young turnips or 4–5 medium ones
10 radishes
8 chive onions or scallions

2 apples
2 small pears
1 lemon
1–2 tablespoons olive oil

1 small bunch of grapes
salt and freshly ground pepper
1 glass of cider
2 handfuls of baby spinach leaves

1 2
3 4

1	Wash the vegetables and scrape or peel them only if necessary.	2	Cut them into roughly even-sized pieces if they are large. Peel the apples and pears, cut them into quarters, and rub with lemon juice.	
3	Heat the oil in a Dutch oven over a medium-high heat. Add in all the vegetables and stir for 3 minutes.	4	Add the fruits, reserving half an apple and half a pear. Allow everything to color, stirring, for 2–3 minutes. Season.	➤

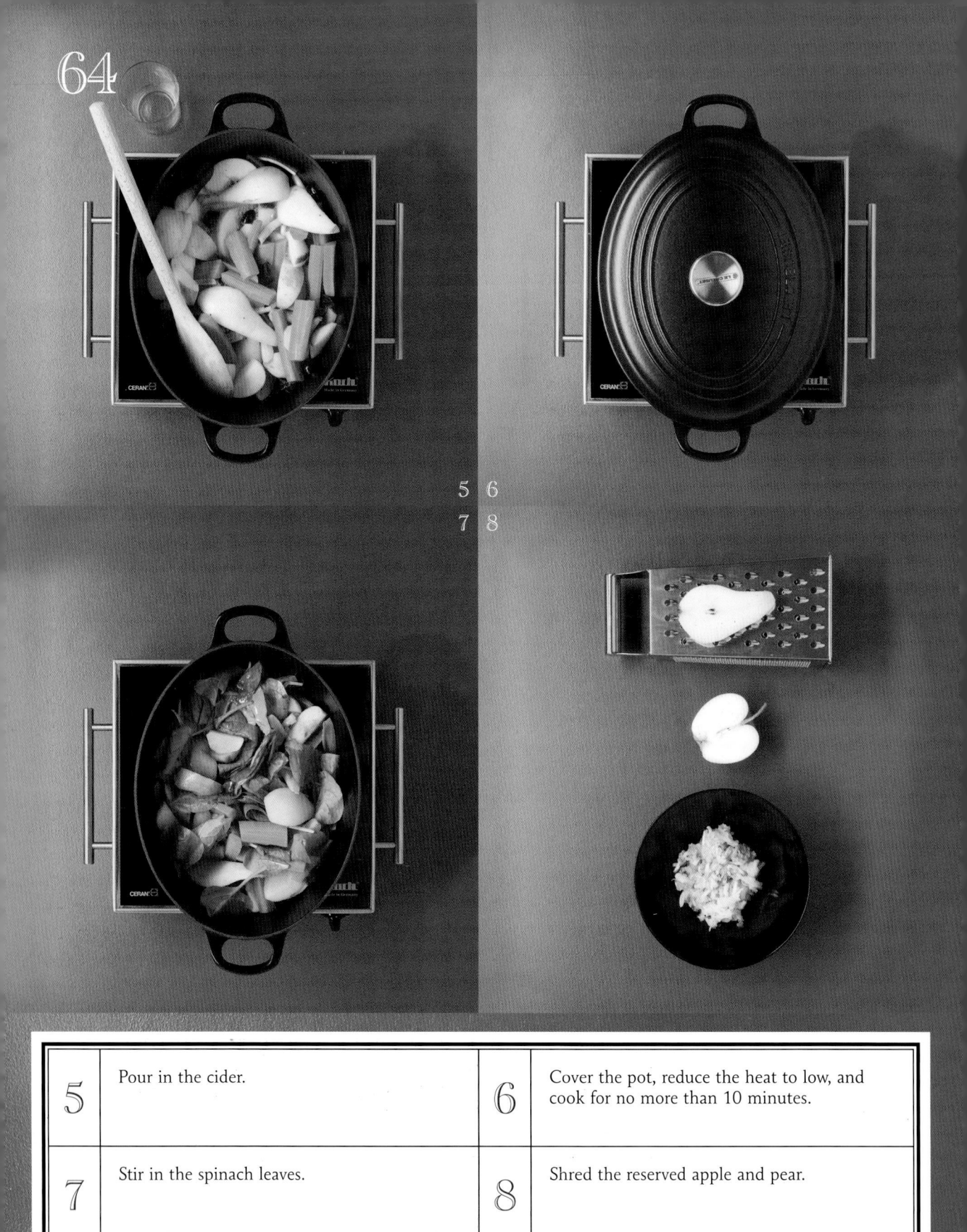

5 6
7 8

5	Pour in the cider.	6	Cover the pot, reduce the heat to low, and cook for no more than 10 minutes.
7	Stir in the spinach leaves.	8	Shred the reserved apple and pear.

9	Add the shredded apple and pear to the dish. It is delicious served with brown rice and a drizzle of olive oil.	**TIP** ☞ Rubbing the quartered apples and pears with lemon juice prevents them from discoloring.
VARIATION		
Use arugula leaves in place of spinach for a more peppery flavor.		

VEGETABLE COUSCOUS

❖ SERVES 6 • PREPARATION: 25 MINUTES • COOKING: 45 MINUTES ❖

3–4 carrots, 3–4 turnips, 3 zucchini
1 slice of pumpkin or butternut squash
2–3 potatoes
2 large onions + 2 garlic cloves
1 orange
3 tablespoons olive oil

½ teaspoon ras-el-hanout
4 cups vegetable stock (2–3 bouillon cubes)
14 oz canned good-quality tomatoes
1 cinnamon stick
1 pinch of saffron threads
10 oz canned garbanzo beans

6 tablespoons golden raisins
1lb medium couscous
2 tablespoons butter
6 tablespoons pine nuts
harissa (smoked chili paste)
½ bunch of flat leaf parsley

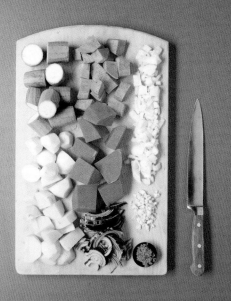

1 2
3 4

1	Wash, peel, and cut the vegetables into large pieces. Finely chop the garlic and pare the rind of the orange.	2	Heat the oil in a stockpot over a medium heat. Add the onion and cook, stirring, for 5 minutes then add the garlic and cook for 1 minute. Add the ras-el-hanout and stir for a further minute.
3	Tip in all the prepared vegetables and stir for 5 minutes.	4	Pour in the stock and the canned tomatoes. Bring to a boil. ➤

5 Put in the cinnamon stick and the saffron, the orange rind, the drained garbanzo beans, and the golden raisins. Let cook for 30 minutes.

❋ QUICK VERSION

You can buy precooked couscous, in which case simply follow the instructions on the pack to prepare it.

❋ THE ADVANTAGE OF A COUSCOUS STEAMER

With this appliance, the meat and vegetables cook underneath, creating a flavored broth that steams the couscous in the basket on top. If the holes in the basket are large, put in a piece of cheesecloth before tipping in the couscous. If you don't have a couscous steamer, use a large stockpot and put a steaming basket on top.

6 7
8 9

6	Prepare the couscous while the vegetables cook: cover the grains with cold water in a bowl and let soak for 10 minutes.	7	Separate the grains using your hands then put the couscous in a steaming basket that will sit on top of the vegetables. Dot little pieces of butter over the top of the couscous.
8	Steam for about 20 minutes, covered with a lid, on top of the vegetables if possible.	9	Serve the vegetables with the broth and the couscous sprinkled with pine nuts (dry roasted in a pan for more flavor) with piquant harissa.

HERBY BULGUR WHEAT SALAD

❖ **SERVES 4** • PREPARATION: 25 MINUTES • RESTING: 15 MINUTES ❖

2 good bunches of flat leaf parsley
1 good bunch of mint
75 g (3 oz) bulgur wheat
2 small cucumbers

1 small red onion
2 tablespoons almonds, skinned and lightly toasted in a skillet
6–8 tablespoons lemon juice (1–2 lemons)

2 tablespoons olive oil or a little more as necessary
salt and freshly ground pepper

99

1 2
3 4

1	Wash and drain the herbs then strip off the leaves.	2	Chop them finely by hand. (You can also chop them in a food-mixer but only briefly, so that they are not chopped too finely.)
3	Cover the bulgur wheat with cold water and let soak for 15 minutes. (Some bulgur wheat needs to be cooked: do check the instructions on the packet.)	4	Peel the cucumbers, cut in half lengthways, and remove the seeds. Cut the halves into small dice. Finely chop the onion. ➤

5

Drain the bulgur wheat and combine all the ingredients in a large salad bowl.

VARIATION

You can of course add 2–3 tomatoes, peeled, deseeded, and cut into small dice.

6 To season: first add the lemon juice. Taste and adjust with salt, pepper, olive oil, and extra lemon juice as required.

SERVING IDEAS
❋

This salad is excellent for a picnic or to serve with a barbecue.

OTHER INGREDIENTS
❋

You can also use large- or medium-grain couscous. But bulgur or cracked wheat has a nutty flavor and a more interesting texture. You need to use mild onions or try with 4–5 scallions.

STIR-FRIED VEGETABLES

❖ **SERVES 1 • PREPARATION: 15 MINUTES • COOKING: 3 MINUTES** ❖

3 silverbeet, including leaves
1 handful shiitake, wild, or cultivated
mushrooms
1 garlic clove
1 small knob of gingerroot

3 scallions
2 tablespoons vegetable oil
1 tablespoon oyster or soy sauce
½ teaspoon cornstarch

IN ADVANCE:
Preheat the oven to 425°F.
Wash the silverbeet.

1	Separate the silverbeet stalks from the leaves. Finely chop everything. Wipe the mushrooms and cut into thin slices. Finely chop the garlic and the peeled gingerroot. Chop the scallions.	2	Heat a wok over the highest heat until hot and smoking. Pour in the oil. Throw in the onions, garlic, and gingerroot and stir-fry rapidly for 30 seconds.
3	Add the silverbeet stalks and the mushrooms and stir-fry, stirring constantly, for 2 minutes. Add the leaves and cook for a further minute.	4	Mix the oyster or soy sauce with the cornstarch and stir into the wok. Let cook for 1 minute and then serve.

JAPANESE TEMPURA

⇥ SERVES 4 • PREPARATION: 20 MINUTES • COOKING: 2 MINUTES ⇤

1 cup iced water
2 cups flour
¼ teaspoon baking powder
oil, for deep frying
salt flakes

selection of vegetables: young celery leaves,
cultivated or wild mushrooms, scallions,
sliced sweet potato or pumpkin, zucchini
flowers, and so forth

IN ADVANCE:
Finely slice all the vegetables and above all
ensure they are completely dry. Heat the oil
in a deep fryer to 375°F.

1	Put the iced water in a salad bowl. Add the flour and the baking powder.	2	Mix together lightly; there should still be some lumps in the batter.	3	When the oil is hot, dip the prepared vegetables in the batter to coat.
4	Drop the coated vegetables in the hot oil. Don't try to cook too many at a time.	5	Turn over the slices after just a few seconds and remove before they brown.	6	Drain on paper towels. Serve immediately with the salt flakes.

DESSERTS

CREAMY

TEATIME

CAKES

FRUITY

EASY RICE PUDDING

❧ **SERVES 4 • PREPARATION: 5 MINUTES • COOKING: 35 MINUTES** ❧

⅔ cup round grain rice
3 cups milk
scant cup crème fraîche or sour cream

1 vanilla bean
1 tablespoon sugar
1 tablespoon butter

VARIATION:
Stir in 1 teaspoon rose water and 1 extra tablespoon sugar at the end.

1	Put the rice, milk, cream, and the vanilla bean in a large saucepan. Add a glass of water and bring to a boil.	2	Lower the heat and cook, uncovered, gently bubbling, for 35 minutes, by which time the rice should be creamy but still slightly "al dente."
3	Add the sugar and the butter.	4	Serve hot or cold.

RHUBARB CRÈME BRÛLÉE

SERVES 4 • PREPARATION: 25 MINUTES • COOKING: 1 HOUR • RESTING: 1 HOUR

10 oz frozen rhubarb
scant cup sugar
1¼ cups heavy cream

scant cup milk
1 vanilla bean
8 egg yolks

IN ADVANCE:
Preheat the oven to 350°.

1 2
3 4

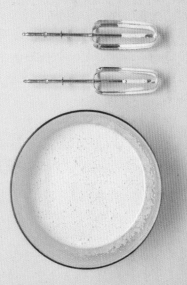

1	Put the rhubarb in an ovenproof dish with 3 tablespoons of the sugar.	2	Transfer to the oven and cook for 30 minutes. Reduce the temperature to 275°F.	
3	Pour the cream and the milk into a pan. Add the vanilla bean, split lengthways, scraping the seeds into the cream/milk mixture. Bring gently to a boil.	4	Beat together the egg yolks with 5 tablespoons of the sugar until the mixture is light and creamy.	➤

5	Whisk in the hot cream/milk a little at a time. Put the ovenproof dish in a larger one filled with hot water to come midway up the sides.	6	Gently pour the custard over the rhubarb. Transfer the dish and its water bath to the oven and cook for 25 minutes.
7	Allow to cool then place in the fridge.	8	When you are ready to serve, preheat the broiler to its highest setting and sprinkle the remaining sugar over the chilled custard.

9	Caramelize the sugar under the hot broiler and serve immediately.	**VARIATION** ※ In place of ordinary sugar, try using raw cane sugar, which is very good caramelized.
TIP ※ The custard needs to be very cold before you flash it under the broiler to caramelize the sugar.		**EQUIPMENT** ※ A regular broiler doesn't always give the best brûlée topping—a specialist cook's blowtorch is ideal for caramelizing sugar.

ITALIAN-STYLE TRIFLE

❖ SERVES 4 • PREPARATION: 30 MINUTES • COOKING: 15 MINUTES • RESTING: OVERNIGHT ❖

1½ cups milk
1 vanilla bean
3 egg yolks

5 tablespoons sugar
2–3 slices of pandoro or panettone
3–4 amaretti (Italian macaroons)
4–5 slices of plain cake

1 glass of muscat and a dash of
Grand Marnier (or other orange liqueur)
1 large punnet raspberries
1¼ cups whipping cream

1 2
3 4

1	First make the custard. Gently heat the milk with the vanilla bean, split lengthways, in a small pan.	2	In a second, larger pan, beat the egg yolks with 4 tablespoons of the sugar.
3	Pour the near-boiling milk over the egg mixture and whisk.	4	Place the pan over a gentle heat and stir constantly until the custard thickens. Set aside and let cool. ➤

5	Line the base of a shallow-sided glass dish with the cake slices. Sprinkle with the muscat and Grand Marnier.	6	Reserving a few to decorate, crush the raspberries with the remaining sugar and spread over the cake.	7	Whip the cream until soft peaks form.
8	Mix one-third of the whipped cream with the cold custard.	9	Spread this mixture over the raspberries.	10	Top with the rest of the whipped cream.

11	Place in the fridge until the following day. When you are ready to serve, decorate with the reserved whole raspberries.	**CHILD-FRIENDLY VERSION** ❈ Use orange juice instead of the alcohol.
	DECORATION ❈	**VARIATIONS** ❈
	A few flaked almonds or candied violets make an attractive alternative decoration.	This is a classic trifle recipe but it also works very well with strawberres and a few slices of banana—dip them in lemon juice to prevent any discoloration.

FLOATING ISLANDS

➤ SERVES 3 • PREPARATION: 15 MINUTES • COOKING: 20 MINUTES ➤

Custard (see recipe 71)
3 egg whites
1 pinch of salt

3 tablespoons sugar
4 cups milk

CARAMEL
2 tablespoons water
3 tablespoons sugar

1 2
3 4

1	First make the custard (follow recipe 71 for the method).	2	Divide between 3 small bowls or ramekin dishes and leave to cool before transferring to the fridge.
3	Put the egg whites in a large bowl with the pinch of salt.	4	Beat the whites into stiff peaks. Add the sugar and beat again. ➤

5 6
7 8

5	Heat the milk in a small pan. When it starts to simmer, reduce the heat to keep it at simmering point. Drop in spoonfuls of egg white and poach for 2 minutes on each side.	6	Remove the poached whites to drain on paper towels then place them on top of the custard in the bowls.
7	Make the caramel: put the water and the sugar in a small pan and heat.	8	As soon as it takes on a golden color, pour it over the floating islands.

		OPTIONS
9	Serve immediately.	❊
		Flavor the milk for the custard as it heats with 2–3 cardamom pods or 2–3 drops of rose water.

HOW TO POACH THE WHITES	VARIATIONS
❊	❊
Drop large spoonfuls of the whisked egg white into the hot milk. After 2 minutes turn them over and leave to cook for a further 2 minutes.	In place of the caramel, decorate the islands with chocolate shavings or crushed praline.

PANCAKES

� SERVES 4 • PREPARATION: 15 MINUTES • COOKING: 30 MINUTES ➢

1 heaping cup sifted flour
pinch of salt
4 eggs

1¼ cups milk
butter, for greasing
sweet butter (optional)

1 2
3 4

1	Put the flour in a large mixing bowl with the pinch of salt. Make a well in the center and break 1 egg into the middle.	2	Mix with a wooden spoon to incorporate the flour into the egg, a little at a time. Do the same with the 3 remaining eggs.
3	Little by little add the milk, whisking to incorporate well.	4	Cover the batter with plastic wrap and let rest in the fridge for at least 1 hour. ➤

73

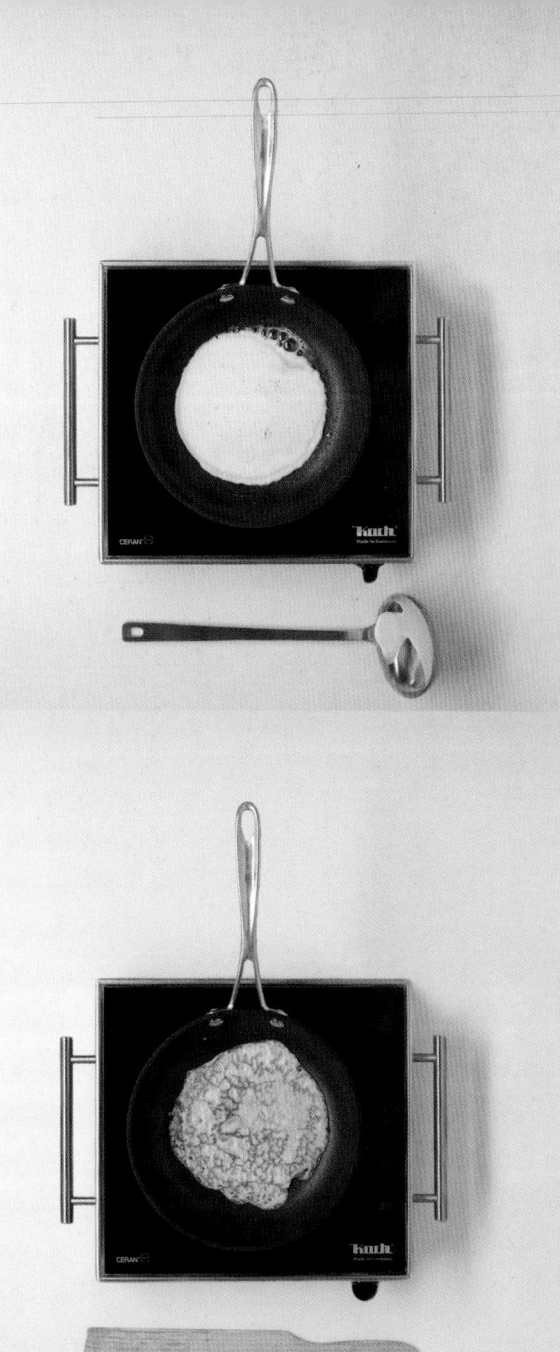

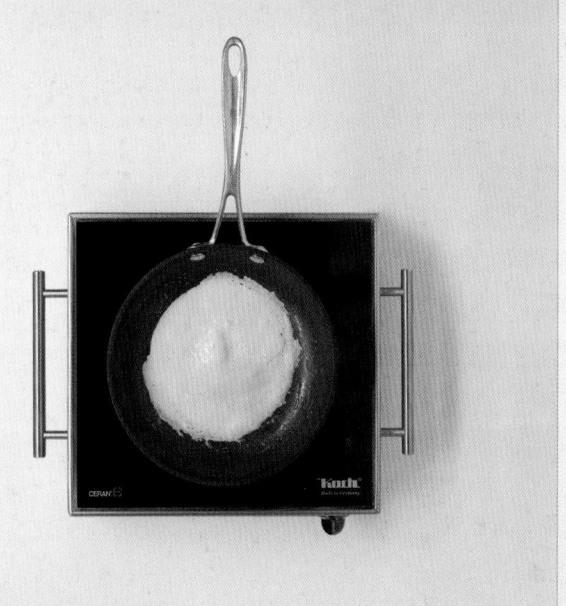

5	Heat an 8-inch nonstick skillet over a high heat. Grease the pan generously with a pat of butter on a sheet of paper towel.	6	Reduce the heat to medium. Pour in a small ladleful of batter.
7	The first side is cooked when the pancake becomes detached from the base of the pan; this takes about 1 minute.	8	Flip the pancake with a quick shake of the pan, or use a wooden slice. The second side cooks in about 30 seconds.

9	Slide out the cooked pancake onto a plate and spread with a little sweet butter if you wish. Grease the pan again with the buttered paper towel before cooking the next pancake. Continue in this way until all the batter is used up.	**TO SERVE** ※ Serve with lemon or orange juice and sugar, or with honey, preserves, chocolate spread, sweetened chestnut purée, and so forth.
		PANCAKE CAKE ※ Layer the pancakes in a large pile with a drizzle of lightly sweetened orange juice between the layers.

EGGY BREAD

❧ SERVES 2 • PREPARATION: 10 MINUTES • COOKING: 6 MINUTES ❧

1 egg
1 glass of milk
1 tablespoon sugar

4 slices of stale brioche (sweet yeast bread)
or soft-batch bread
2 tablespoons butter
1 teaspoon powdered cinnamon

1	Beat the egg in a flat dish. In a second dish mix the milk with ½ teaspoon of sugar.	2	Soak the brioche or bread slices in the sweetened milk.	3	Next dip the slices in the beaten egg.
4	Melt the butter in a small skillet over a medium heat.	5	Fry the dipped slices, one at a time, in the hot butter for about 3 minutes on one side.	6	Flip over the slices, cook for a further 3 minutes, sprinkle with sugar and cinnamon, and serve immediately.

CHEESECAKE

❊ SERVES 6 • PREPARATION: 30 MINUTES • COOKING: 55 MINUTES • RESTING: 1–2 DAYS ❊

5 oz graham crackers or similar
4 tablespoons butter
⅔ cup flaked coconut
3½ cups (1½ lb) cream cheese
⅓ cup sugar

2 tablespoons all-purpose flour
peel and juice of 2 limes and 1 lemon
4 eggs
½ cup crème fraîche or sour cream
1 vanilla bean

IN ADVANCE:
Preheat the oven to 350°F.

75

1 2
3 4

1	Put the crackers into a large polythene bag, tie loosely, and crush the crackers with a rolling pin until they form crumbs.	2	Melt the butter in a small pan, remove from the heat, and mix in the cracker crumbs and flaked coconut.
3	Press this mixture into an 11-inch springform cake pan. Transfer to the oven and cook for 10 minutes.	4	Remove from the oven and reduce the temperature to 275°F. ➤

5	Beat the cream cheese briefly, just until it is smooth, either in a food-mixer or in a large bowl. Incorporate the sugar, then the flour, the citrus peel, and juices.	6	Stir in the eggs, one by one.
7	Add the crème fraîche or sour cream.	8	Pour into the cake pan and transfer to the oven for 45 minutes to 1 hour, by which time the sides should be set but the center still wobbly.

9	Switch off the oven and leave the cheesecake inside for 1 hour then take out and let cool. Remove from the pan and refrigerate overnight.	**SERVING SUGGESTIONS** ✻ Serve the cheesecake with a little raspberry coulis or lemon curd.
OPTION ✻ ☛ The cheesecake is at its best served one or even two days after it is made.		**VARIATION** ✻ For a lighter texture, separate the eggs, add the yolks in step 6, and beat the whites until firm and fold in after the cream in step 7.

PRUNE CLAFOUTIS

❧ **SERVES 4** • **PREPARATION: 10 MINUTES** • **COOKING: 40 MINUTES** ❧

2 cups pitted prunes
1 tablespoon rum
⅔ cup flour
4 eggs
¼ cup sugar + 1 extra tablespoon

scant cup crème fraîche or sour cream
(or light cream for a less rich version)
scant cup milk
pinch of salt
2 tablespoons salted butter

IN ADVANCE:
Soak the prunes in the rum. Preheat the
oven to 400°F.

1 2
3 4

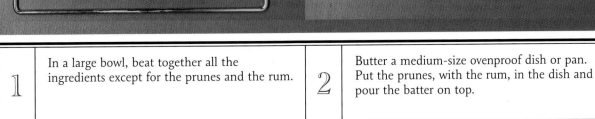

1	In a large bowl, beat together all the ingredients except for the prunes and the rum.	2	Butter a medium-size ovenproof dish or pan. Put the prunes, with the rum, in the dish and pour the batter on top.
3	Transfer to the oven and cook for 40 minutes: the custard should be set and the surface risen and golden brown.	4	As it cools the custard will deflate. Sprinkle the surface with the tablespoon of sugar and serve warm or cold.

RASPBERRY CLAFOUTIS

VARIATION ON PRUNE CLAFOUTIS
❋

☞ Replace the prunes in recipe 76 with 2 punnets of raspberries, and flavor with a few drops of vanilla extract or the seeds scraped from a vanilla bean instead of the rum.

APRICOT CLAFOUTIS

VARIATION ON PRUNE CLAFOUTIS
❋

☛ Replace the prunes in recipe 76 with 1½ cups pitted apricots, and flavor with a few drops of vanilla extract or the seeds scraped from a vanilla bean instead of the rum. Sprinkle with slivered almonds.

BAKED APPLES

→ **SERVES 4** • **PREPARATION:** 10 MINUTES • **COOKING:** 40 MINUTES ←

3 tablespoons salted butter
1 vanilla bean
8–12 dessert apples, preferably Russets

IN ADVANCE:

Preheat the oven to 375°F.

1 | 2
3 | 4

1	Wash and core the apples with a small pointed knife or a corer. Place them in a baking pan.	2	Split the vanilla bean lengthways then cut into pieces. Poke a piece into the core of each apple with a small pat of butter.
3	Transfer to the oven and cook for about 40 minutes. Serve the baked apples just as they are, with a little sour cream or pouring cream.		**TO MAKE COMPOTE** ❋
		4	Scoop out the flesh from the skins with a spoon. Scrape the vanilla seeds from the bean and mix the seeds into the compote with a fork.

APPLE & PEAR CRUMBLE

❧ **SERVES 4** • **PREPARATION: 15 MINUTES** • **COOKING: 35 MINUTES** ❧

1⅓ cups all-purpose flour
½ cup butter
1–2 tablespoons sugar
compote (see recipe 79)
3 pears

4 tablespoons lemon juice
1 vanilla bean (optional)
2 tablespoons slivered almonds
crème fraîche or sour cream to serve

IN ADVANCE:
Preheat the oven to 375°F.

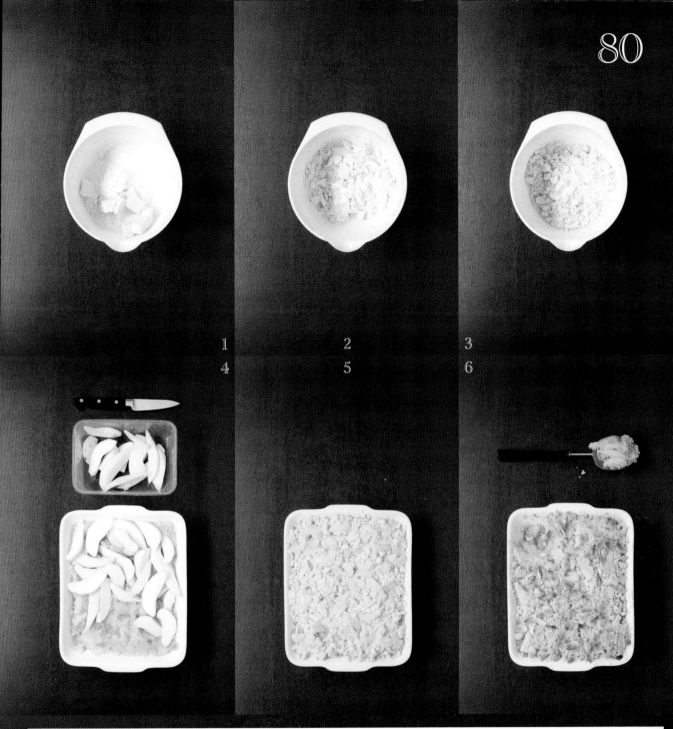

1	Put the flour in a large mixing bowl. Cube the butter and add to the bowl.	2	Rub the butter into the flour using the tips of your fingers.
4	Spread the compote in an ovenproof dish. Scatter with slices of pear and sprinkle with lemon juice.	5	Tuck in a vanilla bean, if using. Spread the crumble mixture over the fruit and scatter with almonds.

3	Add the sugar and stir to incorporate.
6	Transfer to the oven and cook for 35 minutes. Serve with crème fraîche or sour cream.

BALSAMIC STRAWBERRIES

❧ **SERVES 4** • PREPARATION: 10 MINUTES • RESTING: MINIMUM 30 MINUTES ☙

2 punnets of strawberries
3 tablespoons sugar
3 tablespoons balsamic vinegar

1 2
3 4

1	Wash and hull the strawberries.	2	Mix together the sugar and the balsamic vinegar in a large bowl.
3	Cut the strawberries into halves or quarters, depending on size.	4	Put the strawberries in the bowl and gently stir to coat in the balsamic vinegar. Let stand for 30 minutes to 1 hour before serving.

PEARS BELLE-HÉLÈNE

❖ **SERVES 4** • **PREPARATION:** 15 MINUTES • **COOKING:** 20 MINUTES ❖

4–6 perfect pears, not too ripe and
quite firm
2 tablespoons sugar

7 oz chocolate, milk or dark
2 tablespoons crème fraîche or sour cream
vanilla ice cream, to serve

IN ADVANCE:
Peel and core the pears but keep
them whole.

1 2
3 4

1	Heat a medium pan of water with the sugar. When it starts to bubble, add the pears and let poach for about 10 minutes, until the point of a knife pierces them easily.	2	Melt the chocolate in a heat-resistant bowl over a pan of barely simmering water, off the heat.
3	When the chocolate has melted, stir in the crème fraîche or sour cream.	4	Serve the pears with the chocolate sauce and vanilla ice cream.

PEAR & CHOCOLATE TART

✤ **SERVES 4** • PREPARATION: 20 MINUTES • COOKING: 40 MINUTES ✤

butter, for greasing
10 oz prepared Short Pie Pastry (see recipe 08)

3–4 tablespoons sugar
4 ripe pears
3½ oz dark chocolate
½ cup whipping cream
1 egg

IN ADVANCE:
Preheat the oven to 375°F.

THE RECIPE BY STAGES	OPTION
Butter a 9-inch tart pan and sprinkle the base with 2 tablespoons sugar. Roll out the pastry and line the pan. Roughly chop the chocolate and distribute over the pastry. Peel and finely slice the pears. Arrange in spiral fashion over the chocolate. Mix the cream, egg, and 1 tablespoon of sugar and pour over the pears. Transfer to the oven and bake for 30–35 minutes.	Sprinkle the remaining tablespoon of sugar over the cooked tart and caramelize under a hot broiler.
	NOTES
	☛ If you cannot find ripe pears, you can use canned ones or, better still, poach underripe pears yourself (see recipe 82).

APPENDICES

GLOSSARY

TABLE OF CONTENTS

RECIPE INDEX

GENERAL INDEX

ACKNOWLEDGMENTS

GLOSSARY

AL DENTE
An Italian term used to describe the still slightly firm texture of rice grains, pasta, or green beans when there is still a little "bite," that is, not too cooked.

BACON, RINDLESS STREAKY
Good-quality slices should be used in preference to the pre-cubed version sometimes seen.

BAIN-MARIE (WATER BATH)
When you want to cook, melt, or simply heat a dish or an ingredient gently, this is easily achieved by placing a heat-resistant bowl over a pan of gently simmering water (either over the heat or away from it), or by using a specially designed double boiler, or by placing the dish inside another, larger one, which is half-filled with hot water and placed in the oven. The food is, in effect, cooked in a water bath; the heat is very gentle and there is no risk of the ingredients burning or the dish drying out. A bain-marie is perfect for melting chocolate and equally for emulsifying a batter that contains egg yolks (such as sabayon, sauces, and so forth).

BONES
You can remove the bones from a fillet of fish by pulling them out with your fingertips or, better, with a pair of fish tweezers.

BRAISE
This means to cook meat or vegetables in a tightly lidded pot or Dutch oven over a very low heat and in liquid (stock, water, wine, cider…).

BREAD CRUMBS
You can buy ready-made bread crumbs or, better still, make them yourself using stale bread either by whizzing it in a food-mixer or crushing it with a rolling pin. You can also make crumbs using fresh bread but the texture is less even and so not good for coating food such as fish fillets.

BROWN
This means to cook ingredients cut into small pieces over a medium heat in fat or oil. They need to be stirred from time to time to ensure they color evenly on all sides.

BULGUR WHEAT
This is cracked wheat. It has a flavor and texture that is superior to couscous for use in salads.

BUTTER
Salted or sweet, the choice is yours, even for cakes.

CEVICHE
This fish dish originates from South America and consists of raw fish that is "cooked" in lemon or lime juice.

CHANTILLY
This is a cream suitable for piping made from whipping very cold liquid or pouring cream. It is easiest made using a hand-held electric beater but it is possible to whip chantilly with a hand whisk. You can sweeten it and flavor it as you wish (vanilla, Grand Marnier…).

COCONUT MILK
Look for coconut milk sold in cartons, which is creamier and superior to the canned version, which tends to separate. However, if you can only find canned coconut milk, it's easy enough to stir it to a smooth consistency.

CRUMBS
Crumbs are made by rubbing small pieces of butter into flour with your fingertips. The butter must be kept cold and lifting your hands as you work keeps it aerated and therefore cold. You can also make crumbs in a food-mixer fitted with a blade. Put the flour and the cold cubed butter into the bowl and pulse for a few seconds. These crumbs form the basis of shortcrust pastry and crumbles.

MOZZARELLA
Opt for buffalo mozzarella where there is a choice—it has far more flavor.

PANCETTA
An Italian cured meat made from pork belly. It is usually sold thinly sliced.

PANDORO
A traditional Italian sweet yeast bread similar in style to panettone but without raisins and candied fruit. Like panettone, it is usually found in the shops at Christmas time. Use it like sponge cake to soak up alcohol or fruit juice in desserts such as trifle.

POACH
This refers to dropping an ingredient into gently simmering liquid—water, milk, or syrup—to cook it. Poached dishes include fruit such as pears, egg white to make floating islands, and poached egg.

REDUCE
You reduce the volume of a liquid by boiling it to evaporate off some of the water content.

RICE
For rice pudding and risotto make sure you use round grain rice (arborio, vialone nano…). For a pilaf, you need long grain, such as basmati, which is prized for its delicate aroma.

ROAST
This is a method of cooking ingredients (meat, fish steaks, vegetables, fruit, and so forth), either whole or in large pieces, uncovered and without liquid. Roasting is done in the oven, with or without a rotisserie (or over a grill). Often the food is basted with a little fat to glaze and color it, and to prevent it drying out.

ROOT VEGETABLES
Don't underestimate the humble root vegetables! Cleaned and peeled, they are easy to cook and have a delicious flavor.

SEAL
This refers to placing an ingredient (usually meat or fish) in contact with the surface of a very hot frying pan to quickly seal and cook it first on one side and then the other.

SAUTÉ
A term to describe a quick cooking method using either a frying pan or a wok over a medium to high heat, usually with a little fat or oil. The ingredients are generally cut into small pieces and moved around by shaking the pan or stirring the food with a wooden spoon or slice.

SCALE (FISH)
Ask your fishmonger to do this for you.

SIMMER
This means cooking a dish over a very low heat. It will bubble gently.

STOCK
The best stock, of course, is what you make yourself, but when time is short, use good-quality bouillon cubes or powder. Try to find organic bouillon cubes, which have the advantage of being free from artificial flavor enhancers. Allow half a cube for every 17 fl oz of water.

VANILLA
For preference, always choose a vanilla bean (split it into two lengthways and scrape out the sticky seeds with a small spoon or the tip of a knife) or natural vanilla extract. It is far better than vanilla "essence."

WHIPPED EGG WHITE
To successfully whip egg whites, you need to ensure that not the slightest speck of yolk gets into the whites when you separate them and that the bowl and beaters are scrupulously clean and free of any grease. The trick is to whip the whites fast at the end so that they rise in firm peaks. Incorporate the whisked egg whites gently into a mixture so that the air is not knocked out.

TABLE OF CONTENTS

1

CLASSICS

2

PASTA & RICE

3

MEAT

ROASTS

BRAISES

WORLD

4

FISH & SHELLFISH

CLASSICS

PAN-FRIED

MARINATED

5

VEGETABLES

6

DESSERTS

INDEX OF RECIPES

Note: This index is organized by recipe number.

GENERAL INDEX

Note: This index is organized by recipe number.

ACKNOWLEDGMENTS

The author and publishers wish to thank Magimix for the loan of their food-mixers and deep fryer.
www.magimix.com
Customer service : (+33) 01-43-98-36-36

With thanks to the Lucano family.

Props: Emmanuelle Javelle
Design: Alexandre Nicolas
English translation and adaptation: JMS Books llp
Layout: cbdesign